Blossom

Jessica Steidl

1.888.5069-NOW
www.nowscpress.com
@nowscpress

Ordering Information:

Quantity sales. Special discounts are available on quantity purchases by corporations, associations, and others. For details, contact the publisher at the address above.

Orders by U.S. trade bookstores and wholesalers. Please contact: NOW SC Press: Tel: (888) 5069-NOW or visit www.nowscpress.com.

Printed in the United States of America

First Printing, 2017

ISBN: 978-0-9987391-6-8

To God who gave me the words to say.
To my family who encouraged me along the way.
To every girl, may you realize your own beauty and strength through Jesus' love.

Contents

Foreword

This book is for the girl who is lost and afraid. The girl who is hopeful and excited. The girl who is confused and thriving. The girl who is just trying to fit in and make it through. The girl who has dreams. The girl who needs to hear some encouragement. The girl who doesn't have it all together. The girl who is searching. The girl who isn't quite sure about this college thing. And most of all, the girl who wants to stay true to herself and also stay strong in her faith.

If you are that girl, this book is for you. To help you blossom into the woman God has intended you to be. I believe that you were put on this earth for a reason and to do great things. I want to help you tap into that awesomeness already inside you!

I wish I would have had a book like this my freshman year of college, to help me overcome the trials, peer pressure, and experiences I would come across. I want you to be prepared, so that you can have the best college experience possible. Even if you are a senior in college or have already graduated, this book is still for you. These life lessons will help you thrive in each new season of your life. The chapters take you through a journey that ultimately lead you to that peace we all want to feel in life!

Thank you for picking up this book and allowing me to share my heart with you. I have struggled, fallen, and found freedom while at college. I want you to have victory over the trials you face and find that freedom as well! Now, grab your coffee mug and let's chat.

All the best,
Jess

Chapter One
Hope

"For I know the plans I have for you," says the Lord. "They are plans for good and not for disaster, to give you a future and a hope." ~ Jeremiah 29:11

I walked out of my dorm room building, holding a notebook and a folder against my chest. I wore my favorite tank top with white Converse shoes. As I stood at the crosswalk waiting for the light to turn, I watched the waves of students pass by me on their way to the first day of classes at the University of Central Florida. My stomach was a jumble of nerves in this new environment, with new people, new expectations, but above all, I felt one powerful emotion: Hope.

My slate had been wiped clean. As I looked at the students near me, they didn't know me. I could be whoever I wanted to be and do whatever I wanted to do. All this hope bubbled up inside of me as I dreamed about what these next four years of college would be like. The possibilities seemed endless to make new friends, join some clubs, discover my career, and make memories that will last forever.

I went to college two hours away from my hometown. I thought this would give me the perfect amount of freedom, while still being able to drive home on a whim (or when I needed to do my laundry). When I said goodbye to my parents after move-in day and settled down on my freshly made dorm bed, I thought I was so ready to be away.

But oh, how I was wrong. Two hours after settling in, that hope quickly turned into pure panic. I was a wreck. I cried a ridiculous amount in the shower, desperately needing and missing my parents, my home, and my old room. Those cold, cinder block dorm room walls were daunting and unwelcoming.

It took a couple of days for me to adjust, as it probably will for you too, but then after I started classes, I was able to get into a routine, make new friends in my classes, and start to embrace this new adventure. That strong emotion returned: Hope.

I almost wished I had a guide for college that would have taken away the surprises. I'd know my major, who I would be friends with, what my purpose was, and where I was going in the future.

In the end, I'm glad I didn't have anything like that. **The beauty of college is experiencing new things, forming surprise friendships, discovering your passions, and enjoying life.** We don't need to know how everything will play out because our loving God already does. He knows what decisions we'll make, who we will call our life-long friends, and what career we will have! Phew, we don't have to plan it all out because God has already done that.

I asked one of my friends what her two biggest expectations were as she entered her freshman year of college. She thought she would become best friends with her roommate and that her classes were going to be extremely hard. But it turned out to be the exact opposite in both cases. She realized that she wasn't necessarily going to be best friends with the first people she met. And classes are only as hard as you make them because there is so much help that is offered through your teachers, study groups, and tutoring.

Those first few weeks of college are overwhelming, but try not to get caught up in all these grand expectations and miss the experiences right in front of you. Hold on to hope, and try to look at these four years as a chance to step into the person God is leading you to be.

Hope is defined as a feeling of expectation and desire for a certain thing to happen. We have all felt hope like that, especially before a pivotal moment in life, like going to college. You start out so hopeful for what the next four years will bring. They are supposed to be the best years of your life, right? But, there is a lot that you will be faced with during college that will rock you in multiple directions.

Through this book, I want to make you aware of these different trials. I want to help you be prepared, maintain your hope, and come out victorious through Jesus Christ. So, grab your coffee mug and let's talk about how to get the most out of your precious college years!

Think about the prophet Jeremiah; he was filled with hope when he went to Judah to proclaim God's Word. He was doing God's work, after all, and he had been called to do it, so naturally, people would want to hear his message, right? I can imagine him riding into Judah, eager to share the Word.

Except the people in Judah didn't listen to him. They called Jeremiah a failure; they tried to drive him away. How discouraged Jeremiah must have felt. He was in a new territory, just like I was at college, trying to live out

God's plan for his life. Jeremiah couldn't see it at that moment, but God had great plans for him. Jeremiah had hope because he saw the bigger plan. **We can have boundless hope knowing that God is the author of our stories.** He goes with us as we fulfill His mission. We just need to listen and obey. God is holding us in His hands, and He will take care of us. That is where you can find your hope.

God used Jeremiah to bring the people of Judah back to Him. Jeremiah's speeches had a purpose for God's kingdom. We all have a purpose here on this earth. Right now, you were placed at that college for a reason, as part of your path for God. Do not let the enemy tell you that you have made a mistake or you should have gone to a different college, because that will rob you of your precious seed of hope.

Yes, the four years you are embarking on will be challenging. There will be days when you question your choices, days when you want to go home, days when you want to give up. Don't. Look for your hope again. Our God has such a grander plan than we can ever imagine and that plan will surpass your wildest dreams! He will bring you to places you have never dreamed of.

Soak that in. If we can train our mindset to be hopeful, this college thing will be an experience filled with joy! Say goodbye to self-doubt, perfectionism, stress, and control. And welcome our God in. **All it takes is allowing a seed of hope to blossom within you.**

Maintaining that hope

There are three key points I want to share with you on how to maintain your hope through your college years and beyond.

1. The Source

I want you to look up Romans 15:13.

> "I pray that God, the source of ____, will fill you completely with joy and peace because you ____ in Him. Then you will overflow with confident ____ through the power of the Holy Spirit."

I know this is just a fill-in-the-blanks exercise. But the blanks that are there serve a purpose. A purpose of focus. The words you write on those lines will help you remember what is important.

Romans 15 tells us to let God be the **source** of our hope. Joy and peace will all come when we put our trust in the One who loves us and orchestrates our life. When we put God at the center of our life, we will not dwell on all the stress, disappointments, and challenges. We will not let those things destroy us.

Allowing God to be the source of your hope is like a weight off your shoulders. You can finally breathe again! Let that constant worry about what will happen next fly out the window. Doing this will truly change everything in your life. You will have joy knowing that God is a good Father who loves you. The Holy Spirit will fill you with peace, and you will know you're on the right path. You will be hopeful and expectant of the future because you know God has a great plan designed specifically for you!

2. The Living Word

It amazes me every time I read the Bible how many promises and how much hope God gives to us through His Living Word. He has placed it in our hands; we just need to read and receive His truth.

I want you to look up Romans 15:4.

> "Such things were written in the _________ long ago to teach us. And the _________ give us ______ and _______________ as we wait patiently for God's promises to be fulfilled."

Hope will allow you to wait patiently for God's promises in your life to be fulfilled. I encourage you to spend some quiet time in the Bible every day, absorbing all the truth that you can. Maintaining your hope means actively working on it and fueling yourself. **God's promises and faithfulness in the Bible will reaffirm your source of hope day after day.** God has given us the Bible as a tool to bring us closer to Him. Think of it like gasoline. Every day when you get into your car to drive, gasoline fuels the engine so you can go forward. When it runs out of gas, your car will not move.

Much like life, when we are fueling ourselves with God's truth in His Living Word, we will continually move forward. We will be ready and expectant for God's plans to be revealed!

3. Trust

In order to maintain a hopeful spirit, one has to learn to trust God in every area of their life. We have to let go of the reins and trust that God will work everything out for our good, just as Jeremiah 29:11 says.

I want you to look up Proverbs 3:5-6.

> "_____ in the Lord with all your_____; do not depend on your ___ understanding. Seek His Will in ___ you do, and He will show you which path to take."

We don't always do this, and most of us struggle daily with this message. We are, after all, human beings. Young women, who have vulnerable hearts. Emotions and feelings sometimes obscure our understanding.

The definition of "depend" is to rely on. We must rely on God to direct our path in college. I know you will come across many crossroads during your journey, so it is important for you to know who to put your trust in. Trust God with every decision you have to make. He knows what is best for you! That feeling of expectation that is part of the definition of hope can only happen with trust. Ultimately, I know I need to trust God and trust that He will make the way if it is the one I am supposed to travel. It gives me peace when I let go and trust God. I may still get anxious or worry but only for a minute, until I turn my hope back to the Source, which is my loving heavenly Father. Use the Bible as your guide and trust that God will protect you and go with you through every step you take in college!

Everything happens for a reason

When you are faced with challenges in college, which you will be, it is important to remember how to maintain your hope.

I want you to read this next statement with an open mind. Don't skim over the words because you've heard them a million times. Instead, read them with a different, broader mindset:

"Everything happens for a reason."

This statement will bring you peace if you understand "why" everything happens for a reason. **Everything happens for a reason because God has a plan.** It's not just because life is hard. Yes, life here on earth is challenging.

But God has a good plan for your life that should give you hope for a great future.

I know you can remember a time when something didn't go the way you would have liked, but afterward, you realized that it was a blessing.

During the four years I was at college, I learned to have a hopeful mindset in all aspects of my life. This attitude did not happen overnight. It started when I actively drew closer to God.

Even though I have graduated and moved on, I continue to strengthen my relationship with God every day. When I didn't get my "dream job," I remained hopeful. In the end, not getting that job gave me the time to write this book. When it didn't work out with a couple of guys I dated while I was in college, I know it was because God was leading me to my loving fiancé. When I lost touch with one of my girlfriends, I was hopeful that God would lead me to a godly friend who understood me better and was like-minded, and He did.

So, whenever something ended, God blossomed something even better. I put my hope in God because I truly trust Him with my life. He is my best friend. I do not let a breakup or a job denial take away my joy. That joy doesn't come from the world but from God. "I pray that God, the source of hope, will fill you completely with joy and peace because you trust in Him." (Romans 15:13a) That is my prayer for you. I am praying it over you as I write this.

By reading this book, you are already taking a big step in that direction. Now, read on for questions that will help you think about and act on this. Then **decide that you will turn every doubtful thought into a statement of hope.** Doing that will change your life, I promise.

Life Application

Read these Bible verses when you feel like you need more Hope:

- *"Why am I discouraged? Why is my heart so sad? I will put my hope in God! I will praise Him again – my Savior and my God!"* ~ Psalms 42:5-6
- *"Let us hold tightly without wavering to the hope we affirm, for God can be trusted to keep His promise."* ~ Hebrews 10:23
- *"This is why we work hard and continue to struggle, for our hope is in the living God, who is the Savior of all people and particularly of all believers."* ~ 1 Timothy 4:10
- *"Having hope will give you courage. You will be protected and will rest in safety."* ~ Job 11:18

The questions below are for you to connect deeper with God, yourself, and your friends. I encourage you to take some quiet time to get the most out of the journaling questions. When you still yourself before God, oh, my friend, the peace you will feel. The questions for you and a friend will help build relationship, community, and trust. I am so excited for your journey. I pray that college will be a positive experience that will help you blossom into the woman God has designed you to be.

Questions to journal about:

- What are you hopeful for in these next four years of college?

- What does the word "hope" mean to you?
- Has one circumstance in your life made you doubt God?

Questions to discuss with a friend:

- What was your biggest expectation going into college?
- Does your joy come from worldly things, or God?
- Which verse, out of the "Maintaining that Hope" section, was your favorite? And why?

Fun tip for the week:

Write down your dreams this week! Journaling is an excellent way to connect with God and open yourself up to hearing from Him. Having a list of dreams and desires will help you become hopeful when you see that they do come true.

Today, I will trust in Your good, all-powerful name, Jesus. When doubts and worries come into my mind, I will rebuke the enemy's lies and trust in Your truth. I will not lean on my own understanding, knowing that all things work together for my good because I trust in Your name. Thank you for watching over me. Thank you for loving me every minute of each day. I will have boundless hope knowing that my future is bright in Your hands. Please lead me to where You have called me to be.

Amen

Chapter Two
Lies

"Then we will no longer be immature like children. We won't be tossed and blown about by every wind of new teaching. We will not be influenced when people try to trick us with lies so clever they sound like the truth." - Ephesians 4:14

I looked in the mirror, taking in all of the imperfections on my face. The sun was going down, making my room light up with the harsh lights hanging from my ceiling. I could see the frizz in my hair, the random acne on my face, my uneven eyes, my thin lips and makeup that fell short of what I saw in magazines. At that moment, I felt ugly, undesirable, and all the cruel comments from middle school rushed through my mind.

Rationally, I knew I wasn't ugly, but the insecurities that were fostered when I was young kept popping up in my head. My roommate and I were going out to meet some guy friends, and her easy beauty and self-confidence always made me feel overshadowed.

I felt ugly and began to cry. I asked God why I had so many imperfections, why I wasn't as beautiful as my roommate.

Then I paused and took a deep breath. Those are all lies. My beauty wasn't the same as my roommate's, because I wasn't her. God loved me as I was, and that meant I needed to learn to love myself too.

The enemy

The devil is the father of lies (John 8:44). He is the one who plants those seeds of doubt, insecurity, and failure. The voice in your head telling you to stop trying. He will do whatever it takes to bury your spirit and leave you as a fearful, unhappy person.

Who wants to live like that?

The enemy's sole purpose is to drive a wedge between you and God. He wants you to doubt God and believe that He doesn't care about you or that you are somehow of less value in His eyes. John 10:10 talks about how the enemy comes to seek, kill, and destroy. That might sound harsh, but it is true. We must understand that the devil is real, and demons are real. Every day, we wage a spiritual warfare because we are followers of Christ.

That is why it is so important to do what 1 Peter 5:8-9a says, "Stay alert! Watch out for your great enemy, the devil. He prowls around like a roaring lion, looking for someone to devour. Stand firm against him, and be strong in your faith." Resist. Resist. Resist.

I know how hard that can be. The pressure of school, of work, of complicated relationships, coupled with your inner doubts about how capable you are can make you want to quit. All you want to do is give up, hide in your bed and binge on TV. Don't. When we are tired, it is easier for the devil to work his deception. We are too exhausted to fight back, and **one small lie will lead to a bigger lie and so on until your self-esteem is at the bottom of a pit.**

The misery brews in those spaces of depression and isolation. By not resisting, you are essentially allowing the enemy to have a full advantage on the battlefield. Once the enemy sees that he has deceived you with a small lie, he will come back with his cavalry.

Those lies form the basis of doubt, which can debilitate you or make you hesitate in pursuing your goals. Sometimes it's hard not to give into the doubt you feel while you are at college. We are faced with many life decisions, and sometimes we don't feel equipped or strong enough to make the right choice. Once we start doubting ourselves though, and more importantly, God, we are on a quick spiral downward. Doubt builds like a snowball going down a hill, and if you let it grow big enough, you'll hesitate in taking risks in life or going after your dreams.

Those doubting, self-disparaging thoughts are not from God. We all need to learn to be alert for these thoughts and be prepared with Scripture and faith as our armor. Then we can let those lies go and start to move forward, toward the amazing life that God has planned for us.

Perfect image

My legs are fat. My hair is too frizzy. My major is dumb. I'm not smart enough, pretty enough, nice enough.

These are some of the lies we tell ourselves. We can be so judgmental, more so of ourselves than we are of others! We are truly our own worst critic. And how sad is that? We are perfect in God's eyes, yet we rarely are in our own. We need to identify ourselves in Jesus, not in this world and its perceptions of beauty and humanity.

Society has made us believe we have to be the "perfect" girl. My friend said that she struggled all throughout college with thinking that she had to be the girl that every boy desired, the one most in shape, the funniest person in the room, and the smartest in her classes.

Do you feel this way too? Are you feeling exhausted with all the effort and worry it takes to be "perfect?" Your mind gets caught in this revolving spiral, obsessing over your outward appearance, your personality, and your flaws. Because of that, you are never content, never truly happy.

Think of that one person in your group who frets about everything, and no matter how much you reassure her, she still worries about her hair, her face, her clothes. No amount of compliments or kind words will make her stop feeling less than—because knowing that you are perfect exactly as you are, with all your flaws, comes from within. From seeing yourself how God sees you. Imperfect, messy and yet still amazing in His eyes.

My friend said freshman year should really be called "the fitting in year." It's true. You spend that whole year finding your place in an all-new world, and figuring out who you are now that you're an adult. It can be almost impossible not to feel inadequate, until you learn to look to God for reassurance that you are already perfect in His eyes.

The Power of Social Media

Social media compounds these feelings and gives the enemy a continual avenue to feed our self-doubts. I do most of my own negative self-comparing on social media. I'll see some girls who look perfect on Instagram and start to feel some envy and insecurities.

We like to tell ourselves that our friends have it all. That the image they are portraying on social media is "perfect." They work out more, have more friends, go out more often. You start to base your worth on how many followers you have and if you are posting cute pictures.

Stop and ask yourself, why do you think they are so perfect? What makes them have this image to you? Could it be that they're hiding their insecurities by posting what seems like the "perfect" picture? A picture they may have agonized over for hours with different poses and filters and editing? **A picture is a flicker of time, not an accurate depiction of life.**

Once you peel back the layers on a social media picture, you will discover a person whose life is not perfect. They worry in front of the mirror. They stress in the middle of a test. They get needy or depressed. They feel like they are failing. They have things that terrify them and things that make them cry when they are alone. That big show on social media is not real life.

I have learned to push past feeling like I wasn't living up to those impossible standards by stopping those thoughts at the source. I curtailed the time I spent on social media, and whenever a negative thought arose, I refocused my mind on being happy for the other person instead of tearing myself down.

I surround myself with people who make me feel beautiful by building me up when I express an insecurity. These Christian women remind me where I should put my worth, in Jesus Christ. They help direct me back to our God who made us in His image—an image which is perfect by the way.

You have to remember that the enemy wants to keep you in a state of wishing you were somebody else, instead of embracing who you really are. Do your awkward social encounters leave you hating yourself? Do you ever see strangers, and wish you looked like them? I have been there and know how those comparisons can cycle in your head, making you doubt yourself and stay mired in lies that you are not good enough.

The enemy wants you to remain in that dark place of wishing you had someone else's personality, financial situation, family dynamic, looks—whatever. If he can keep you in this state, you will constantly seek after the things you don't have, and never be truly satisfied with who you are.

Choose to believe what God says about you. Resist spending time focusing on your weaknesses and insecurities. I want you to stop saying things like "I am not as good as ___" "I am less than ___." You need to change those "I am" statements into positive affirmations—I am smart. I am capable. I am strong. I am loved by God.

I encourage you to see yourself as God sees you: forgiven, blameless, His child, beautiful, and loved. **God's opinion is the only one that should matter.** Your identity doesn't depend on what you have done or will do. It resounds in who God says you are.

Once you choose to follow Jesus and to believe the truths He whispers in your ear; you become a new creation. You stop living from a place of what other people say you are, and take hold of the truth of God's Word.

I want you to look up **2 Corinthians 12:9-10.**
"For when I am ___, then I am ___."

When we waver and feel inadequate, not worthy, or not good enough, that is when we must depend more upon God. When doubt weakens us, our God is so strong. He is our source of strength every single day, but especially when we are struggling. Once we stop believing the worst about ourselves, we can start experiencing the greatness God has for us.

You will experience so much joy in this life when you learn to love the person God created you to be, in every aspect of yourself. God created you to be unique and special on purpose. How boring would it be if we all looked and acted the same?

If you refocus your attention on God, the transformation you will see in yourself will be amazing. This image to be perfect will hopefully keep decreasing as the months go on. One of my best friends said it beautifully:

Comparison is the thief of joy, and I have never struggled more with something so true. Every day those thoughts attack me and tell me I am not good enough, not smart enough, not popular enough, not pretty enough. Every one of those is a lie, and I know it, but how does it all continue to haunt me?

The devil sees the weakest portions of my life, and he grabs onto them. He pokes at the wounds, brings light to my insecurities, and stops at nothing to bring me down. Don't let that happen.

If you have ever felt unworthy, you are not alone. Every single day I have to remind myself that I am unique and created with love in the image of God. He thinks that I am so precious and special and loves me, so He sent His only Son to die for me.

When you are feeling unworthy, unloved or lonely, cling to the one hope that we have in this life—that Jesus Christ made every soul unique. He loves the way your eyes wrinkle when you smile, the little flyaway hairs on your head that you find annoying, the way your laughter fills an empty room. He loves all of you, every little bit, and that will never stop.

Don't let the devil win. Don't give him the satisfaction of pushing you down. Push back, get up, and tell him that you are beautiful just the way you are. You have a purpose, and

God has a plan for your life that no one else can fulfill. So rise to the occasion, take action, love yourself, and tackle the plans God has made for you.

You are enough.

When the enemy is attacking your insecurities, confidence, and self-worth remember that last statement above. **You are enough, worthy enough in the Lord's eyes.** For when you feel weak look to God for your strength. Philippians 4:13 says, "For I can do everything through Christ, who gives me strength." Jesus has given us the power to rebuke the enemy's lies. Use this power daily, meditating on the verses below!

Life Application

Read these verses when you need a reminder of your own power:

- *"Jesus called His twelve disciples together and gave them authority to cast out evil spirits and to heal every kind of disease and illness."* - Matthew 10:1
- *"No, despite all these things, overwhelming victory is ours through Christ, who loved us. And I am convinced that nothing can ever separate us from God's love."* - Romans 8:37-38a
- *"When the seventy-two disciples returned, they joyfully reported to Him, 'Lord, even the demons obey us when we use Your name!' 'Yes,' He told them, 'I saw Satan fall from heaven like lightning! Look, I have given you authority over all the power of the enemy, and you can walk among snakes and scorpions and crush them. Nothing will injure you.'"* - Luke 10:17-19
- *"No power in the sky above or in the earth below – indeed, nothing in all creation will ever be able to separate us from the love of God that is revealed in Christ Jesus our Lord."* - Romans 8:39

Questions to journal about:

- What is one lie you believe about yourself?
- What is one lie you tell other people?

- What is one lie the enemy is making you believe right now?

Questions to discuss with a friend:

- Are you struggling with believing a lie right now?
- Do your friends make you think you have to be perfect?
- Do your friends speak truth over you or lies?

Fun tip for the week:

This week I want you to write down every lie that either the enemy is telling you, you are telling yourself, or you are telling someone else. I then want you to cross through every lie. Say out loud: I will no longer believe this. It is important to identify the lies that you might not even realize, and the ones which consume your thoughts. Then counter those lies with truth. Instead of "I'm so fat," say to yourself, "I have a strong, amazing body." Free yourself this week!

Today, I will wear the Shield of Faith to protect myself against the enemy's fiery arrows of doubt, temptation, and setbacks. Proclaiming every day that You are a mighty God. I will use the Sword of the Spirit to counter the enemy's lies and gain ground for Christ's kingdom. I will only speak words of encouragement today to myself and others. In the precious name of Jesus, I will learn to love myself in a better way by falling more in love with You, Father.

Amen

Chapter Three
Despair

"We are pressed on every side by troubles, but we are not crushed. We are perplexed, but not driven to despair. We are hunted down, but never abandoned by God. We get knocked down, but we are not destroyed." ~ 2 Corinthians 4:8-9

More often than you think, you will be wandering around during college, maybe actually lost because the campus is so big, or lost in your search for a purpose, a career, and an identity. It's almost like being a lost sheep. "If a man has a hundred sheep and one of them gets lost, what will he do?" Jesus said in Luke 15:4b. "Won't he leave the ninety-nine others in the wilderness and go search for the one that is lost until he finds it?" That story is a parable for us—we are Jesus' flock. And just as He would find a lost sheep, He will do the same for you. He will constantly go after your heart until you let Him in, and then He will guide your path. He will never leave you behind, to wander around lost by yourself.

I can recall many times in college when I struggled with my purpose and identity. I felt spiritually lost. What does God want me to do with my life? What is my purpose here on earth? Should I be doing more? Who am I as a woman of Christ? What is my identity?

If you have asked yourself any of these questions, you are not alone. College is a pivotal time in a young woman's life, because we get the chance to discover who we are. Free at college, living on our own, away from our parents, and taking those first steps toward a career. Those decisions are scary and big, and some of us follow what others do, rather than striking out on our own.

It is easy to feel despair in those moments. To feel lost, alone, and helpless. Faith is about believing in what we cannot see, and there will be times in your life where your faith falters because you can't see God standing beside you. Despair can overwhelm you, paralyze you, keep you from living and loving your life. Hold on…there are ways to combat those feelings and bring yourself back around to strength and joy.

Disappointments

Disappointments will come in big and small forms throughout college and life, and in those moments when it seems that all is lost, we can fall into a state of despair. We do not have to be defeated by setbacks. **Try to remember that disappointment often stems from unrealistic expectations.** We want more than what we have, and when we don't have it, disappointment settles in.

When you were a little kid, you probably wished for a particular toy. When you were a teenager, you looked to friends, a boy, or a new car to make you content and happy. When you got to college, you think doing it all: a sorority, good grades, clubs, and finding a husband will make your life mean something. When you graduate, it's all about finding the best job, getting married, or buying another car to replace your old one. The "needs" continue to escalate, and when we don't receive those things, then disappointment can easily edge into despair and those thoughts of *I'm never going to get a good job. I'm going to be in debt forever. I'm going to be stuck in this awful apartment.*

Do you see the problem here? Those kinds of thoughts are about the lack of things, when the real lack is in your faith. Where is God? Are you actually content and happy when you base those emotions on achievements and possessions? No. Because there will always be another new and shiny toy to chase. **Contentment comes from within, not from outside of yourself.**

The most frequent disappointments for me during college came from my friends. I had to learn that I couldn't expect too much out of people. They are human just like me, with their own sinful natures. The fact is, you will be let down, you will get hurt, you will be left alone sometimes. What you do about those situations is what is important.

I used to put too much of my joy into my friend's hands. I gave them the control over my emotions and mood. If they liked me or included me or called me often, I was happy. When they didn't, I was depressed. This was a dangerous place to be. I came to realize this as disappointment after disappointment happened.

It hurts to be left out. I get that. I would look at my Snapchat and Instagram feeds and see some of my friends together having fun at an amusement park and realize I had been left out. I was never invited. I took it personally, which would leave me in a state of despair. Maybe my friends didn't like me. Maybe I wasn't fun enough…

It was a vicious circle that did nothing but undermine my joy. Finally, I got mad at myself for being so affected by something out of my control, and decided I had to shift my thinking. To pull myself out of that state of despair by looking to God.

No matter how big or small a disappointment may be—from not being invited to a party, to losing your dream job—we must remember where to put our joy. If we put it in external things, we will be weighed down when things don't go the way we expect.

On this earth, our joy has to come from the Lord, the only One who will truly satisfy our souls. We do not have to wallow in our disappointments and let them bring us to a dark place.

When something doesn't go the way I want it to, I give myself a minute to entertain the disappointment I'm facing. That's it—one minute. Then I stop and think about the source of those negative feelings. I know that God has plans to prosper me and not to harm me (Jeremiah 29:11), which means those emotions of despair are coming from the enemy. Why would I want to allow the devil to whisper inside of my head? After that minute is up, I breathe the negativity out of me with a deep breath and let it go to God. I then forgive whoever has disappointed me. I do not let bitterness reside in my heart. I forgive them and then move forward.

Sometimes I choose to meditate on Psalm 28:7, "The Lord is my strength and shield. I trust Him with all my heart. He helps me, and my heart is filled with joy. I burst out in songs of thanksgiving."

You have to make a choice every day to decide what you will allow to affect your day or not affect it. I choose to put my joy, hope, and trust in God. When a disappointment comes my way, I do my minute-pity-party and then get on with my day! I refocus my eyes on what makes me happy, which is knowing how much God loves me and that the path He has planned for me will be better than anything I could have planned for myself.

Loneliness

Another component of despair is loneliness. When you go to college, you are stepping into a new world, often one that is far from all the people and places you know. You become convinced that you are alone. You have no friends. God doesn't hear your cries. You think you have no one to turn to. I have been there, and so have some of my friends.

There have been many times in my life when I have experienced all three of these feelings: loneliness, abandonment, and disappointment. One of my friends told me recently that she went through a long period of that.

My mom passed away from a cancerous brain tumor when I was 15 years old. The days, months, and years that followed were full of these unwanted feelings. The pain I felt after losing my mom to cancer is hard to even put into words. The word "lonely" seems like an understatement. My whole life changed in one day, and I no longer had my best friend, mentor, and caretaker in my life.

These feelings of loneliness extended beyond just the loss of a mother. It was not long after she was gone that I began to feel like my dad was gone too. Shortly after my mom passed away, my dad filled the void in his heart by dating a new woman I had never met. He began to bury himself in work, he rarely engaged in conversation about my mom, and he seldom came home. I was disappointed that my dad would choose to be so distant during a time when my sister and I needed him most.

This disappointment gradually led to a deep feeling of loneliness and sadness. A year after my mom passed away, my sister went off to college, and I was more alone than ever before. She was my only sense of refuge during that first year without Mom and Dad around. As a 16-year-old girl, I felt like I was facing life alone. After weeks and months of coming home from school to an empty house, I decided to load my car with some of my belongings and stay with a friend for a while. After a few months of this, I chose to go back home and focus more on my relationship with my dad. Through much heartache and tears during this season, I grew up along the way and trusted God in the process.

Overall, I have to believe that deep down, my dad was just lost and did not know how to cope with the death of his wife. However, seven years have passed, and things have not really changed much. Early on, it would have been hard for me to say that I was "abandoned." The word "abandoned" carries a negative connotation and is not something that I would ever want to be defined as. However, when I look back at the last seven years, whether I like it or not, that is exactly what I was.

My friend, however, has not let all of this impact her zest for life. She has heartache, but she has chosen to live with joy and gratitude. I asked her how she overcame those feelings of despair and she said it was simple—through her faith: ***God has walked alongside me during the most painful days of my life, and I know that He is capable of restoring and healing me.***

One verse that has encouraged me is Ephesians 3:20 which says, "Now all glory to God, who is able, through His mighty power at work within us, to accomplish infinitely more than we might ask or think." I hold onto this promise daily as I continue to walk hand in hand with Jesus. I still have hard days, but this verse gives me hope that He continues to work within me even when He seems distant.

That hope that we talked about in Chapter One has carried my friend through her hardest days. She knows that God was with her through it all, because she felt Him in the special friends He had brought into her life just when she needed them most, in the strength inside her to forgive, and in the blessing of a sister who faces the world with her.

Through the despair, God was blossoming her into the woman she is today. Strong, inspiring, and brave. Allow Him to do this in your life! Whether it is your identity you are struggling with, or a huge disappointment you can't get over, or true loneliness, lay it all down at the feet of Jesus. Once you do that, you will be able to move forward, towards the future God has planned for you!

Life Application

Here are some verses to really meditate on. Let them wash away your insecurities. We can find our true identity in Christ if we look and listen to His Word:

- *"Even before He made the world, God loved us and chose us in Christ to be holy and without fault in His eyes."* ~ Ephesians 1:4
- *"And when you believed in Christ, He identified you as His own by giving you the Holy Spirit, whom He promised long ago."* ~ Ephesians 1:13b
- *"For we are God's masterpiece. He created us anew in Christ Jesus, so we can do the good things He planned for us long ago."* ~ Ephesians 2:10
- *"So you also are complete through your union with Christ, who is the head over every ruler and authority."* ~ Colossians 2:10
- *"God has united you with Christ Jesus. For our benefit, God made Him to be wisdom itself. Christ made us right with God; He made us pure and holy, and He freed us from sin."* ~ 1 Corinthians 1:30

Questions to journal about:

- How do you deal with a disappointment?
- Have you felt abandoned? Do you blame God?
- Do you feel like God is always with you?

Questions to discuss with a friend:

- Did you feel lost in those first few weeks of school?
- What was the biggest disappointment when you got to college?
- Have you had a moment of despair? How did you get through it?

Fun tip for the week:

This week I want you to write on your bathroom mirror (with dry erase markers, which are easy to wipe away): "I am a princess of the One True King!" Keep it up there for as long as you need. Read it out loud every day, until you believe that in your heart.

Lord, I release this despair in my heart into Your hands. I don't want it anymore. I pray that You will fill me with Your strength to approach each new day with a restored spirit. Thank you for walking through life with me. I pray that I will feel Your presence, Lord, in all my moments of struggle.

Amen

Chapter Four
Weakness

"So I say, let the Holy Spirit guide your lives. Then you won't be doing what your sinful nature craves."
~ Galatians 5:16

College puts an enormous amount of pressure on you. There are so many expectations, tasks, and worries. One day a professor is assigning a 40-page paper, the next day you're loaded up with reading material. Then one of your friends has a crisis with her boyfriend and needs you. And now, suddenly, you feel weak. This load is too heavy to bear, and you don't think you have the strength to meet the challenges before you. The enemy loves it when you're stressed, on edge, and one moment away from losing it. Your priorities will shift away from God and towards the pleasures of this world if you choose to seek refuge in procrastinating or partying.

Some people thrive off of being busy and being around other people. But if you're like me, you might desperately need time to be alone. It helps me to recharge, refocus, and relax. I call it my triple R-time.

Whatever category you fall into, **in those moments when you feel that the world is crashing down around you, find a happy place to retreat to, a place where God is at the center.**

Overwhelming Responsibilities

In college, I felt like I was the only one doing homework. My friends knew where to find me, on my comfy brown couch with a Literature book in one hand and a highlighter in the other. On top of reading numerous chapters each week, I had mini essays to write, discussion postings to respond to, and papers to analyze. I never felt like I was ahead in my school work, I always felt two assignments behind.

Can you relate?

Meanwhile, my roommates were at the gym or watching Netflix or hanging out with other people. I envied their free time and felt the pressure of all the responsibilities of meeting deadlines and maintaining good grades mounting on my shoulders. Each new task weighed me down, making me weak with worry and fear that I'd fail.

I not only had the pressure to do well in class, but I also had to go to volleyball practice twice a week from 9:30 p.m. to 11:30 p.m. I'd go back to my dorm, mentally and physically exhausted. Most of my weekends were spent at volleyball tournaments, some far away and some close. In between all that, I worked part-time and tried to maintain a social life. By Sunday night, I was so overwhelmed that I wanted to just sleep for a week.

I struggle with pressures and how they affect me. Do you?

I didn't and still don't always handle it well. When I have a lot going on in my life, and I don't feel like I have time to breathe or time to myself, I get so overwhelmed that I eventually hit my breaking point. For me, the stress would drive me to procrastinate, which would only make things worse.

The pressures of college hit me hard and left me crying in my bed desperately wanting peace, free time, and my cat Bella. I would keep my stress bottled up inside until it exploded like one of those water bottles used in science experiments.

I'd look at my schedule and not see a moment to have a Netflix night at home or a slow morning to enjoy sipping my coffee and having quiet time with Jesus. This would make me grow more anxious, and send my mind into overdrive.

I'd hit these breaking points about once a month. Instead of moving forward, I would dwell on all the things going wrong in my life, the things I didn't have, and stress over all the things left on my To-Do list. All of these felt like cinder blocks, each one weighing me down, sinking me deeper into a dark hole.

I wasn't making enough time for God during those first years of college. He got pushed aside in my planner behind all of the other pressures that filled its pages. Yet, He was the only One who could restore my spirit and get me out of the state I was in. It took me far too long to realize that.

Now I have learned to cry out to God in the midst of my struggles and pressures. I've learned it's okay not to have it all together, to get stressed over homework, and to feel overwhelmed. Don't be afraid to reach out to your loving God or a trusted friend. Talking about your burdens and worries eases the stress inside of you. I know you may feel like you are burdening them or complaining. Remember that everyone goes through this, everyone has stresses of their own, and thus they can relate and give you a much-needed hug.

Above all, I want you to give yourself grace. **Forgive yourself for moments of weakness, for those moments of doubt, for sometimes buckling under the pressure.**

I had to do this when I chose to stop playing club volleyball in my last semester of college. I needed to free up my schedule and focus on what was important in my life, and when guilt hit me about quitting the team, I paused and extended kindness toward myself.

Take time right now to evaluate your current calendar of pressures. Are you handling everything well? Are you pushing things that are important to the sidelines?

When you find yourself in this place, remember Psalm 61:2-3: "From the ends of the earth, I cry to You for help when my heart is overwhelmed. Lead me to the towering rock of safety, for You are my safe refuge, a fortress where my enemies cannot reach me."

When we feel overwhelmed, bombarded by the pressures of life, weakened under those burdens, we need to cry out to our heavenly Father.

The Lord knew before He created us that we would have times when we felt overwhelmed and weak. He knew that we would need a day of rest, thus creating the Sabbath. "Keep the Sabbath day holy. Don't pursue your own interests on that day but enjoy the Sabbath and speak of it with delight as the Lord's holy day. Honor the Sabbath in everything you do on that day, and don't follow your own desires or talk idly." (Isaiah 58:13) How wonderful that God gave us a day each week to spend in worship, rest, and refresh for the next week. Don't look at Sundays as another day to do more things—look at it as a day to recharge.

When we take time to rest, we refocus our attention on God. The Holy Spirit's power helps us create boundaries, breathing room, and quiet time. Finding rest and contentment in college is essential to living a less stressful and more fulfilled life, and for giving you the ability to experience college in a deep, enriching way.

When you take time to rest, to shrug off the burdens that weigh you down, joy will fill your whole being, and you will start to enjoy your freedom. Freedom to do what you want, to say no to people or plans, to take time to honor God, and to use the Sabbath as a day of rest. It's not weak to say no—it's the opposite. It's standing strong in your convictions and in your trust in God's Word. **The more you stand on your own rock, the more you will find the inner strength to serve you when times get tough.**

Peer Pressure

One thing you won't be able to escape here on this earth is peer pressure. We live in a fallen world, which means we are all sinners and continue to sin every day. Some people take on the instigator role, and others are compliant.

We must be so careful with this one, especially in college. I know what it's like to want to fit in with the "cool kids." This is a worldly desire that so many of us have a hard time turning our backs on. To be accepted by fellow peers in college, there's an unwritten rule that one must drink, smoke, sleep around, or wear skimpy clothes. The pressure is continuous—*everyone is doing it,* you hear. *It's not that big of a deal.* But it is, especially if it compromises who you are and who you want to be.

But I know what you're saying, peer pressure can be really hard at times to resist. Especially if it comes from your closest friends.

During my freshman year at college, I was not where I am today in my faith. I couldn't find a church I liked; therefore I was not always the best at watching sermons online or reading my Bible. Because of this, I would justify the mistakes I made by comparing them to other people. I wanted to have friends, so I would go where they went, even if it meant staying out too late when I had an early class the next morning. The "cool" thing as you may have already experienced is to drink. People would say you weren't fun if you didn't. So, I would carry around a drink to look cool but barely took a sip, as I was underage and knew this was wrong. I would wake up the next morning with guilt trying to break me down. I knew in my heart that I wasn't being myself, I wasn't this person who went out this much and wore crop tops, but I felt weak. Unwilling to trade my friends for my values.

I reached a point during my sophomore year that I decided to stop just talking the talk, and start walking the walk. Meaning, I did not want people to hear that I was a Christian with shock on their face because they saw me out at the bar last night, or heard me cuss on the volleyball court. I put old behaviors, peer pressures you can call them, behind me. I moved toward Jesus' shining light. I wanted to truly live a life that showed Jesus through my actions. I was reminded of strong women in my life, like my mom and my sister, to make good choices and to stand up for my faith.

The greatest advice I can give to help you resist peer pressure, is to surround yourself with people who hold the same values and commitment that you do. I wish I did this sooner, back in my freshman year. The earlier you do this in college, the less worldly sorrow you will have. It is all about who you call your close friends and spend a lot of time with. "Show me your friends, and I'll show you your future," is what my Pastor Kurt Parker always says. And it couldn't be truer.

The people we associate ourselves with influence our daily decisions. You may think you will stay on the straight path, continue being a "good girl," but the more you entertain temptations and surround yourself with tempters, the easier it will be to cave. Our guard will slowly fall; the enemy's lies will start to sound like the truth. *Drinking isn't bad unless I get drunk. Smoking weed isn't horrible for you. She's doing something so much worse, so I'm good.*

Having like-minded friends will help you not fall into peer pressure. It works both ways—if you hang around with someone who has a negative influence, it's easier to be influenced by them. They cuss, so you start to add in a cuss word here and there. They take a shot, so you do too. They gossip, so you start finding yourself gossiping more. Sometimes we do this without even realizing it. That is the type of influence that people we view as friends can have over our lives.

I want you to understand that God views all sin in the same way. If you tell a white lie or if you are sexually immoral, it is all still a sin to God. So the, "Oh, well my drinking often isn't as bad as her sleeping over at her boyfriend's house every night" comparison isn't going to fly. All sin separates us from God. To get back to Him, we must go to the Word of God and find the truth.

The good news is that God will forgive you. No matter what you have done, He will forgive you. All we have to do is repent and ask for forgiveness. We have freedom from sin's grasp in Jesus' name.

"Sin is no longer your master, for you no longer live under the requirements of the law. Instead, you live under **the freedom of God's grace**." (Romans 6:14)

No matter the peer pressure you have fallen into, **God is there to be your rope out of sin's dark hole.** He is so ready to wash you white as snow when you repent to Him. So, do not think that you are in too deep. There is a way, and His name is Jesus!

Place your box full of regret and mistakes at Jesus' doorstep. Ring the doorbell, and turn to leave. He will take them from you. How awesome is that?

Life Application

Verses to help you overcome Weakness:

- *"So Christ has truly set us free. Now make sure that you stay free, and don't get tied up again in slavery to the law."* - Galatians 5:1
- *"God is my strong fortress, and He makes my way perfect."* - 2 Samuel 22:33
- *"Let us go right into the presence of God with sincere hearts fully trusting Him. For our guilty consciences have been sprinkled with Christ's blood to make us clean, and our bodies have been washed with pure water."* - Hebrews 10:22
- *"Instead, clothe yourself with the presence of the Lord Jesus Christ. And don't let yourself think about ways to indulge your evil desires."* - Romans 13:14

Questions to journal about:

- What pressure do you need to free yourself from?
- Do you have regrets from those first few months or years of college?
- What do you need to repent to God right now?

Questions to discuss with a friend:

- Do you have blank spaces in your schedule?
- Can you relate to being so overwhelmed? How do you cope with it?

❀ What type of peer pressure do you struggle with?

Fun Tip for the week:

If you don't have a planner, go out and buy one. Or you can make a planner out of notebook paper. I want you to create space in your schedule to connect with God, with a close friend, and refresh yourself. Plan to spend time in nature, go to a bookstore, or cozy up in your bed with your Bible. I am so excited for you to experience the peace that can come from the Holy Spirit! Be at rest and restored this week.

I come humbly before You now, Jesus. I give You _____. It has been weighing on my heart, and I need to repent. I ask for the forgiveness that I have been promised through accepting You as my Lord and Savior. I pray that You will keep me on the path of peace and life. Please help me to create breathing rooms in my life. I ask the Holy Spirit right now to fill me with peace and restore my anxious heart. I pray that You will give me wisdom and strength to fight off the temptations of this world. With Your help, I will stand firm in my morals and faith, Lord. In You, I know that I have victory over the enemy. Thank you for never leaving me, and for forgiving me. I love You, Lord.

Amen

Chapter Five
Fear

"For God has not given us a spirit of fear and timidity, but of power, love, and self-discipline."
~ 2 Timothy 1:7

Although it may seem like a common fear, I would say that my biggest fear is being hurt. I am afraid of good things going away, I am afraid of being disappointed, and I am afraid of things that I cannot control. To protect myself against these fears, I have built mental and emotional walls. I have pushed people away, and I have hidden from things that seem "good" or "happy." After being hurt and disappointed time and time again, it sometimes can be hard to envision a different ending.

I went through a series of painful events over the last seven years. After being disappointed and abandoned over and over again, I became accustomed to these feelings. I convinced myself that I was fine, and I started expecting the worst in all situations. If I expected the worst, then I would never be disappointed (I was basically in a constant state of preparation for whatever came my way). This protective mechanism eventually made all my emotions stale and flat.

Happiness is not safe. Happiness is a risk. That risk is scary because I do not want to know what it feels like to lose happiness again. Too often, we are afraid of loss, and so we guard against that by not allowing ourselves to be vulnerable and happy. However, I am learning that it's okay to be happy and that God wants that for me! He wants me to experience joy and feel worthy of that, so I am continuing to work on putting value in myself and to overcome fear before it overcomes me.

Fear of Abandonment

My friend shared that story above with me one day, and I remember thinking how much I could relate. Unfortunately, our past has a way of getting into our future. Past disappointments and past heartache have made us fear abandonment. We fear that somebody is going to leave us, or that we may lose something precious.

Have you felt fear like that before?

I know I did while I was in college. I would meet new people and think they could become close friends, then we'd drift apart, and I'd be left feeling hurt. I built up those walls like my friend did because I didn't want to get hurt again, by anyone. I would talk to a guy I was interested in, then a few weeks later, he'd go back to his ex-girlfriend. It happened three times…no lie. I began to feel like I wasn't good enough.

Unfortunately, we take these past hurts and pain into our new relationships. It creates a fear of trust, of falling in love, of being vulnerable. We become afraid to put our hearts out there, in constant worry that the person will leave.

When I met my fiancé, I told myself I was done talking to boys. I needed to give my heart a break. But when God ordains a meeting, He makes it happen.

That's what happened with Jacob. I remember praying to God; please protect my heart Lord, I don't want to get hurt again. Please remove me from this situation with Jacob now if it is not meant to be.

For six months, I kept my walls up and guarded my heart. I needed time, and Jacob understood. It wasn't until I learned to trust Jacob that I let go of that fear of abandonment and let him see the real me.

I was only able to get to this point by ultimately trusting in God. When I let go of the tight hold of my heart and put it in God's hands, I felt the peace that I was supposed to pursue Jacob with a purpose.

For me, there is a profound difference when I am in a friendship or relationship that has a purpose. For friendships, I have found other young women that share a common love of Christ. These girls didn't leave. They were constantly there to pray for me, offer encouragement, and hang out with me so that we could both resist some peer pressures.

For my relationship with Jacob, we both had the common goal of dating with a purpose and future in mind. This helped the fear I had at the start of our relationship fade away. We would bring up the future often, and it felt good to know where he saw things going and that we were on the same page.

If you felt that God-ordained meeting with a person, then trust that it will work out. Even if the time is not now, but later. We all have experienced the pain of people leaving, but many times we forget that God has a purpose for everything and that He can see the path ahead.

I want to challenge you to allow God's perfect love to cast out all your fears. Only then are we able to receive what God desires for us. To do this, we must place our fears in God's hands. Be honest with God what is worrying your heart, and say, "This fear is too much for me to handle. I surrender it to You, Lord, because I trust that You are good and will take it." Exchange your fear for God's love. Even though it is an uneven exchange, that is how God intends for it to be. Because He loves us more than we can ever understand or grasp in this life.

Fear of Failure

You know when you have a big moment or life-changing decision coming up, and you are filled with hope and excitement. But, there is something else there. Fear. You fear that you will fail. Your moment has finally come, but you start to pull back some. You don't want to be a failure, so why try, right?

Oh, how I have felt this constant, restless fear during college. I changed my major a lot throughout college, so therefore I always thought I was a failure. I would have a negative mindset towards my new major, thinking I was going to fail before even getting started. My past failures would weigh me down, and try to keep me stuck in that place of doubting myself and God. You could say I was truly setting myself up for failure.

Have you done this?

My friend shared her viewpoint on fear with me:

Ever since I can remember, it has been my dream to open up a bakery. It's not always easy to follow your heart and your dreams, though. Doubt gets in the way, big time. For me, I doubt myself, my capabilities, and my path, all of it. I think sometimes; I doubt that I am even chasing after something that God had set out for me to do.

But when I feel this and when I doubt, those are the times that I have to completely stop, saturate myself in truth and revert to what I know is instilled in the depths of my heart. It's easy to get stuck in that fear of uncertainty and just allow that to be an excuse for not moving forward. But being willing to try is all you need.

So often I feel lost, but all I can do is continue to have enough courage just to continue to place one foot in front of the other and allow Jesus to guide my steps. For me, it is better to have tried and failed than to have never tried and wonder what could have happened. Even the biggest failure beats never having the courage just to try. (Stay tuned for her full story in the next chapter)

A lot of big things happen during college, like your career choice, relationships, grades and it's important not to fear that you are going to fail, but to believe in yourself and your capabilities. To believe that everything will be okay. My friend felt that uncertainty about her career, and she feared what the outcome would be. Would she fail or would her bakery be the best one in town? The thing is that we do not know because **we are not called to. Only God knows.** Remember in Chapter One, we talked about not trusting in our own understanding, but in God's promise to direct us on the right path (Proverbs 3:5-6). Because He knows what is best for us!

In the Bible, Moses is an example of someone who was afraid of failing, because he could not speak well. He did not think he was capable of talking to Pharaoh about releasing his people. I can just picture God saying, "Challenge accepted." Even though Moses viewed himself as inadequate, God saw him as the chosen one. There was a time when Moses was trying to handle this fear all on his own. He was leaning on his own understanding instead of God's. Moses made excuses because he feared he would fail at this big job. "But Moses pleaded with the Lord, 'O Lord, I'm not very good with words. I have never been, and I'm not now, even though You have spoken to me. I get tongue-tied, and my words get tangled.' Then the Lord asked Moses, 'Who makes a person's mouth? Who decides whether people speak or do not speak, hear or do not hear, see or do not see? Is it not I, the Lord? Now go! I will be with you as you speak, and I will instruct you in what to say.'" (Exodus 4:10-12)

God challenged Moses to believe in His power. God was able and willing to give Moses the right words to say, so he had nothing to worry about. Easier said than done, I know. It is easy for us to focus on our weaknesses when faced with big decisions, but if God is calling you to do something, then He will help you do it. All we need to do is ask for help. And then trust and allow God to provide you with the strength, courage, and ability to succeed.

Are you letting this fear of failure stop you from doing something? Are you making excuses for yourself as Moses did?

When I would get my papers back from my teachers in college, their harsh comments would make me feel like a failure. I had to remind myself to have confidence in my abilities. Writing is my passion, and I'm still going to do it, I just have a lot to learn. I had to believe in myself and believe that I was capable of succeeding. I worked harder on my next paper and continued to see improvement.

I do not fear failing anymore because I believe in the abilities and talents God has given me. I am hopeful that He will pick me back up and lead me towards the place that I will succeed. **I am not a failure in God's eyes when I am following His Will.** God was with Moses and fulfilled His Will for his life, and God will do the same in our lives.

In college, we must not give up when we fail once. Because you may fail again. Through those shortcomings, we must remain hopeful and trust that God will still fulfill His plan for our lives, just like He did for Moses. There is no need to fear failing because God is there to catch us and push us in the right direction. We must have courage as we take new opportunities, and try new things. Have a feeling of excitement, instead of failure.

What do you do when you fail? Will you give up, or try again? Life is sometimes like trial and error. We must try new things to find out what we are good at. Stay hopeful that God's plan for your life is still in motion.

The book of Proverbs reads like a poem about many topics, but especially on success and hard work. I suggest reading and meditating on one chapter every day. There are 31 chapters, which will take you through the month. There is so much wisdom in those chapters. The repetition of reading similar truths every single day helped me believe what God was saying in Proverbs.

By the end of that month, I challenge you to see the transformation of your mindset. I believe it will be one that lets what is in the past stay there. You move forward without fear, trusting that everything happens for a reason. You view times that you may fall as room for growth.

Life Application:

Some key verses when you need to release your Fear:

- *"Give your burdens to the Lord, and He will take care of you. He will not permit the godly to slip and fall."* - Psalm 55:22
- *"I prayed to the Lord, and He answered me. He freed me from all my fears."* - Psalm 34:4
- *"Don't be afraid, for I am with you. Don't be discouraged, for I am your God. I will strengthen you and help you. I will hold you up with my victorious right hand."* - Isaiah 41:10
- *"Do not be afraid or discouraged, for the Lord will personally go ahead of you. He will be with you; He will neither fail you nor abandon you."* - Deuteronomy 31:8

Questions to journal about:

- What are your deepest fears?
- Where do you think your fear is coming from?
- What steps can you take today to help you overcome your fear? Tomorrow? Create an action plan.

Questions to discuss with a friend:

- What are you afraid to surrender to God?
- What part of the future do you fear?

- Do you struggle with the fear of failure? How do you deal with that?

Fun tip for the week:

This week I want you to write one fear on a notecard. On the other side of the card write down a verse that speaks truth against your fear. Write as many notecards as you want. Keep this note card in your car, backpack, or tape it to your bathroom mirror and when you feel that fear, recite the Scripture on the back. Actively work on freeing yourself from your fears with God's Word!

Jesus, reveal to me right now what fears I am holding onto. What do You want me to surrender to You? Lord, You never intended for us to have a spirit of fear. I pray that I will trust everything in my life to Your precious name. I want to have a faith like Abraham. To live in reverent fear of You, Lord, every single day. Seeking Your will above my own. I am confessing my fear of ______ to You today. I welcome Your love and freedom. I renounce the enemy's hold on this fear in the name of Jesus Christ. I pray You will give me a spirit of love and confidence. Thank you for sending Your Son to die for me because I can now receive the freedom Jesus gave me every single day.

Amen

Chapter Six
Courage

"Be strong and courageous, and do the work. Don't be afraid or discouraged, for the Lord God; my God is with you. He will not fail you or forsake you."
~ 1 Chronicles 28:20a

My friend has shared a memory with me so many times, it almost seems like I'm reading a novel when I hear it. She talks about how she could see the light peeking through the blinds in her kitchen window. Her mother's cookbook was lying out on the counter, it was another early morning spent baking. She was a little girl again, in the kitchen with her mom. Flour fights, trying new recipes, and eating way too much icing. She still thinks about that picture of herself as a two-year-old, sitting on the kitchen counter in her diaper covered in flour, helping her mom bake cookies. They could spend the whole morning and afternoon getting lost in the ingredients and laughter. Those special moments forever lived in her heart. It had been seven years since her mom passed away.

This deep passion for baking has been so present throughout her entire life. The kitchen had become her haven. It was her getaway and breath of fresh air. Nothing brought her as much excitement as when she got to try out a new recipe.

Her dream has always been to open up a bakery of her very own with her mother's recipes. In her senior year of college, she was all set to go to graduate school to pursue a different route. An open door for baking at a local restaurant has now lead to an open door to having her own bakery shop one day.

With courage, my friend is running through the open door that God has placed in her path. Knowing the risks and instability of what she is doing, her passion and trust in God continue to drive her to her lifelong dream.

Let's face it, having courage is hard. For me, chasing my dream of opening a bakery is scary because it not safe. It's risky. People will often tell you that your dreams are 'too risky.' Those words can be hard to hear; especially when they come from someone you look up to. For me, this is my dad. He is completely success driven and always pushing me to go after the "safe and secure, making good money" option. Pursuing a career in baking is the screaming opposite of that.

But, there comes the point in my life where I have to decide for myself and stand firm in my belief that Jesus has placed this passion in my heart for a reason. I need to face the doubts and the insecurities and push through the fear of the unknown to get to where I want to be. ***Courage is about feeling that fear that frightens you and doing it anyway!***

My courageous friend decided to push past that fear of failure, and overcome it with God's truths. It is scary, risky, and the success of her bakery shop is not guaranteed. But, she believes in her heart that God will bless her because she is following His Will for her life.

Can you relate to this?

Courage is defined as the ability to do something that frightens you. Fear is the opposite of that definition. Fear is the voice in our ear telling us that we can't climb that mountain, ace that math test, perform at our recital, or be in a relationship. You might not realize it, but you use courage every day to make life decisions. Courage is the fuel that helps you live your life to the fullest. Courage is what pushes you past the fear and gives you the strength to take a leap of faith even when you can't see what's on the other side.

Courage is also defined as strength in the face of pain or grief. The enemy wants you to wallow in your pain, not battle it back with strength and overcome the dark days. This strength that drives our courage comes from God. He calls us not to be afraid or discouraged.

> Look up **Joshua 1:9.** "Be _______ and __________. Do not be ______; do not be __________, for the Lord your God will be with you ________ ____ ___."

God wants to remind us that He is always with us. There is no reason to be terrified or discouraged because He is beside us. "Be strong and courageous," God says.

I know it might be hard to do that when you are lost, alone or have just suffered a devastating loss. The waiting periods from the dark to light can seem endless. Grief, fear, depression are all like black holes that suck you deeper the longer you stay in them. Something little can be that last straw, and suddenly you begin to doubt God. Is He still here? Does He hear me? Let me encourage you today. Yes, God is always with you and hears your every cry. He has commanded us in that verse not to be discouraged because He is standing beside us to guide us to a better place.

Have you ever taken a step back and looked at a situation? In that moment you maybe felt like God didn't hear your many, many prayers about a job or a loved one with cancer or a scary moment in your own life. I have not always had courage, and by allowing myself to stay stuck in the fear and darkness, I've almost missed everything going on around me. I had to really ask myself, what is God trying to show me right now? What is He trying to tell me?

I want you to ask yourself those questions right now if you are experiencing a waiting period or a moment of doubt and fear. **Have hope, be courageous and move forward, because God has a wonderful life for you, just around the corner.**

Opportunities

I am a dedicated fan of the show *So You Think You Can Dance*. I have danced most of my life, which makes me connect with the dancers and routines. For those of you who don't know about this amazing show, the dancers have to go through an audition in front of three judges. Once they impress the judges, they get sent to "The Academy." In this current season I am watching, there are ten All-Stars (top dancers from previous seasons) who have the final say on who they want to dance with on the show. Only ten dancers will make the live show out of one hundred. Talk about a challenge!

Each week, another dancer is sent home. Poof. Their moment of fame or career break-through is taken away from them in a second. They all know that this could happen at any moment, yet the dancers show up, practice after practice, show after show, brave enough to get on that stage and try.

You can see that courage in the short interviews they do with the dancers before they leave. Their responses, at a moment of severe disappointment, always inspire me. "As a dancer, we hear the word no every day, but I'm not gonna give up. I'll be back," one of them said. I admire their courage, their ability to keep going after those opportunities, to keep risking rejection.

It's not just about courage—it's about hard work. Those dancers work out daily, practice constantly, and learn everything they can about their craft. No matter the big break you may be waiting on, it will take dedication and time. It won't be handed to you on a silver platter. It may not happen when you want it to, so continue to work hard and wait for the right opportunity and in the meantime, be courageous enough to walk through the doors that open before you.

When God offers you opportunities, will you take them? Even if it is not in your timing?

I want you to really think about this because you will face this during college and the rest of your life.

My friend was recently given the opportunity to get a new job that would be closer to her house, offer her more benefits, better pay, and good career advancement. Still, my friend was anxious. She wasn't ready to leave the comfort of her old job, where she had friendly co-workers and felt a part of a team. God was opening the door wide open for her, but yet she resisted.

My friend could have decided to stay at her current job, and wait for another opportunity to arise down the road. Instead, she took that leap of faith and followed God's direction. She trusted that if God was going to give her this new job, then it was the right move for her to make. She knew that this was God's plan because she felt peace about her decision. All the worries and doubts were gone. She has been receiving the blessings at her new job because she feels she is where God intended her to be.

What a beautiful story that we all can take something from. Waiting is hard. We can sometimes get complacent waiting around, just living life day by day. It's scary when you have to go outside of your comfort zone and make changes.

Even with this book that is in your hands right now, I had to take an opportunity that was given to me, without knowing all of the answers or knowing for sure if it was the right time. But I did know that I had to take that leap of faith no matter what. God was giving me the opportunity to follow my dream, and I wasn't going to let fear or doubt stop me.

I want you to have this attitude when faced with milestone opportunities during your journey. Follow the open doors that God gives you. Be patient in the waiting seasons, knowing that "good things come to those who wait." Use those waiting periods as the time to work harder at your craft, grow, and better yourself. So that when your opportunity arises, you will be ready!

Esther

Esther is an inspiring example in the Bible of a courageous woman. She risked her life to save her people. She cared more about her people than her own security. Even though Esther was a queen, she still had to be invited into the presence of the king. "If you keep quiet at a time like this, deliverance and relief for the Jews will arise from some other place, but you and your relatives will die. Who knows if perhaps you were made queen for such a time as this?" (Esther 4:14)

God prepared the place and opportunity for Esther, and she chose to act, knowing that it could mean risking her own life. "And then, though it is against the law, I will go in to see the king. If I must die, I must die." (Esther 4:16b)

With careful planning, Esther asked the king for two banquets. God was working behind the scenes, setting things in place for when Esther would tell the king of Haman's plan against the Jews (Read Esther for the full story; it is awesome). Because of Queen Esther's courageous act, a whole nation was saved. She set aside her own fear and trusted in God. She relied on Him for her security, not the status of the crown.

What a compelling story. How many of us would risk our own life for others?? Are you putting too much of your security in worldly things instead of God? Esther could have chosen to make endless excuses about how the king would never listen to her. She could have let her fear overshadow her courage. We can learn from Esther's courageous act when we are faced with a difficult decision. My Life Application Study Bible lists four key points that you can use to make decisions in moments like this:

1. *Calculate the cost.* Esther understood that she could lose her life.
2. *Set priorities.* She put her own life behind the safety of the Jewish people.
3. *Prepare.* She sought support and encouragement from her people and fasted about the decision she had to make.
4. *Determine a course of action and move ahead boldly.* Esther knew what she had to do, and with courage, she took action without thinking about it too long.

In my life, whenever I have a big life decision ahead of me I take the necessary time to evaluate and listen to God. It is not courageous to make quick decisions that you will later regret. Courage does not take away the fact that you need to plan carefully. It is important to learn from Esther so that you can also seize God-given opportunities.

God puts us through trials in life, not to discourage or terrify us, but to help us learn how to have courage and strength. But, God promises us that He is there every step of the way. He truly knows what's best because He is in control of our lives. We need to have faith and trust that there is a reason for our wait or our pain. This waiting period I am going through now is not destroying me. I am excited for what God has planned! Because of that, I can truly enjoy living in the present moment, not worrying about tomorrow or months down the road. Matthew 6:34 says not to worry about tomorrow because each day has enough trouble of its own.

You will be faced with many difficult decisions during your college journey. I encourage you to do what is uncomfortable. Take risks, with the needed planning, that God will place in your path. Remember to put your safety and security in God, and not in your own resources on this earth. God is the only One who can intervene and deliver us.

Life Application

Verses to help you find Courage:

- *"So we can say with confidence, 'The Lord is my helper, so I will have no fear. What can mere people do to me?'"* - Hebrews 13:6
- *"They do not fear bad news; they confidently trust the Lord to care for them. They are confident and fearless and can face their foes triumphantly."* - Psalms 112:7
- *"So be strong and courageous, all you who put your hope in the Lord!"* - Psalms 31:24
- *"Be on guard. Stand firm in the faith. Be courageous. Be strong. And do everything with love."* - 1 Corinthians 16:13-14

Questions to journal about:

- Was there a moment in your life when you needed to be courageous? What did you learn from that?
- Do you take risks in life? Why or why not?
- Do you trust God with your future career? Spouse? Home?

Questions to discuss with a friend:

- Is there an opportunity right now that you need to take?
- How can you relate to Esther? What would you have done in that moment?

- ❀ Do you hold security in your possessions or in God?

Fun tip for the week

Go on an adventure this week! Somewhere you have never gone before. It could be a day of paddle boarding or a visit to an amusement park. Take a friend with you and have a fun, adventurous day!

Lord give me a courageous spirit today, to do the things that scare me. In Your name, I pray that I will pursue the dreams You have placed on my heart. Knowing that if it is from You, then it is good. I vow to live a life that is pleasing to You. I pray that You will lead me to Christian women who share the same love for You as I do. I want to build up my community so that I can courageously stand firm in my faith. I love You, Lord. I will boldly go forward today not fearing the things I can't see. Because I know, You'll go before me, and You're with me right now. Thank you, Lord.

Amen

Chapter Seven
Strength

"Be strong and courageous, for you are the one who will lead these people to possess all the land I swore to their ancestors I would give them. Be strong and very courageous. Be careful to obey all the instructions Moses gave you. Do not deviate from them, turning either to the right or to the left. Then you will be successful in everything you do."
~ Joshua 1:6-7

Joshua was chosen to lead the Israelites into the Promised Land after Moses passed away. Not only did he have to lead them there, but he also had to conquer this strange new land. Talk about a challenging job! Without God, this would have been frightening and quite impossible. But obeying God meant he had God with him as he embarked on this adventure. He drew his strength from the knowledge that God would be with him wherever he went.

College can often be a strange new land for us. Even if you go to school close to home, a big university can seem daunting. We don't know a lot of people and we might walk alone to class for a while, and thus feel alone and scared.

I remember sitting on the lawn looking at my campus's huge fountain. It was a sunny, warm fall day and I watched swarms of students pass by me, friends chatting, laughing, all in tiny worlds of their own, a world I was still on the periphery of because I'd yet to make any real connections at school. At that moment I desperately wanted to climb into my car and go home, and maybe never come back. I wanted to be in the place I felt confident in, not this overwhelming, scary new place.

I started to get up when a girl I had never seen before sat down next to me. "Are you in American Literature? Sorry, don't mean to be creepy but I saw your book sitting there."

I told her I was, and that the class was kicking my butt. "Me too, the stories are so hard to follow. Which teacher do you have?"

Hearing her say that she was struggling too kept me from getting in my car that day. Her admission of weakness became a source of strength for me. We talked for an hour or so about our class, then college in general, and then I walked away with a new friend. I thanked God for placing that girl in my path when I needed her the most. **Look around you—the strength you need may already be right beside you.**

Staying on Course

We talked about peer pressure in Chapter Four, but I want to talk about another pressure that college will bring. Once we are on our own, we don't have the structural strength from our parents anymore to have a curfew, follow the rules, or stay true to our values. It's very easy to fall away from your principles, depending on how strong the pressure can be.

My friend shared with me that she really struggled with the pressures she felt from guys and her friends during college: *I shifted away from my faith in college because I didn't want "limitations" on my social life. I became a "go with the flow" person. I would be at the bar with my friends, not caring how many shots of alcohol I had to take to impress this guy that I liked. I didn't care about the consequences that I knew would come in the form of a hangover the next morning.*

I pushed that out of my mind so that I could take more shots and "have fun" in the moment. But, the next day after I went out, I did absolutely nothing. I was like a blob on the couch. My head spun, I could still feel the alcohol in my veins, and I just felt crappy overall. You know what I would do though? Go right back out again the next night. I didn't take responsibility for my actions, and I did things in those moments of intoxication that I am not proud of. I got sucked in deep to the party scene, and I resisted the voices in my head telling me to stop.

All this built-up guilt and regret hit me all at once one morning. I thought about the years that I had been so concerned with doing what everyone else was doing, and in that process, I was losing sight of myself. I thought I was a terrible person and that there was no way to come back from the things I had done.

It was my senior year, and I could see this road of destruction I was headed down. I sought out a church and vowed to turn things around. It felt so good to be back in this warm, welcoming space with God. I could feel Him speaking to me through each sermon. He refocused my eyes on the important things in my life like my relationship with God, showing kindness to others, and the family and friends I am blessed with. I repented of my past sins, and I allowed

Jesus' love to wash away all of my guilt. Since I know God forgives me, I was able to forgive myself.

That realization and the actions she took afterward required incredible inner strength. It is far harder to swim against the current than with it, but knowing that others have done that, it can inspire you with strength, too. I want to share one more story with you:

My first two years of college, I played volleyball for a local state college. I quickly made friends with my teammates and loved getting to live in an apartment with some of them. They would often go out and party on the weekends, and it started to look like a lot of fun. They were always waking up the next morning with these massive headaches, but they always had funny stories to share about their crazy night.

I began to feel like I was missing out on the fun. Then, one evening I got invited to go to my first party with them. I went into my room immediately thinking about the perfect outfit to wear. About an hour or two before we were going to leave, I felt a little nudge in my heart. I sat down on my bed with my comfy sweatshirt on and thought about why I was going to this party. I was trying to be like my teammates. I was trying to be like every other college kid. And for what?

As Christians, we are called to be different. The more I thought about it, the less I wanted to go. I did not go to that party because I realized I didn't want to be like everyone else. I wanted my life to be a reflection of my heart. A heart that loves God and is pursuing a deep relationship with Him. Yes, it was a huge step to say no. But honestly, I am so happy that I did. Instead of going to that party I was able to spend the weekend with my best friends from home, kayaking on the river, and soaking up God's creation with others who shared a heart for the Lord.

God and the people who love me deserve my time way more than those people I didn't even know at that party.

I share those two stories with you to tell you that you are not alone in this. These are two real-life people who have been up against the same pressures as you have or will be. I want you to understand that **our faith does not put limitations on having fun during college. Instead, we can rely on it for our strength when those difficult choices arise.**

Being a Christian does not mean we are boring people who stay at home reading our Bibles all day. We identify ourselves in Jesus, not with how much we can drink or how many times we went out last week. This new identity changes everything.

The Bible tells us to work with a clear head. "Stay alert! Watch out for your great enemy, the devil. He prowls around like a roaring lion, looking for someone to devour." (1 Peter 5:8) God gave us this Scripture to help us prevent mistakes from happening when we drink too much and are not in the right state of mind. There is a reason He has called us to live a different life. When our mind is distorted, we are more susceptible to do things we will later regret. It just isn't wise. Going to a party, or having a glass of wine doesn't make you a bad person. However, when you put yourself in a precarious position, it's really easy to fall off the edge. One drink can lead to two or ten and then a lot of bad decisions.

It takes courage to go against what your friends are doing. You're in a new place, you're alone, and that creates a position of weakness. So you end up at a party, and these new friends are offering you alcohol or drugs. It would be so easy to say yes, to fit in, to become part of that world. You wouldn't be alone anymore. You'd have lots of friends, a community.

Think for a moment. Are those the friends you want? People who make poor decisions, people who encourage you to go against your values? When I choose friends, I do it with one criteria—are these people who will make me a better person? If the answer is no, then walk away.

Believe me; I have had that mental wrestling match between those two sets of friends often: Christian friends and my "Fun" friends. I didn't always make the right choices during my freshman and sophomore years, and I remember standing at a party one time thinking *this isn't me. I'm not being my true self.* I had to distance myself from those people, which wasn't easy.

All of my friends knew me as the girl who didn't drink much, who was always the DD (designated driver). It was a target on my back. My own friends would say things like, "It's my goal this semester to see Jess get drunk." "Why are you being so lame?" I was looked down upon because I did not get wasted on a weekly basis.

I fell into the trap of conforming in those early years because I was not secure in who I was in Christ. I was scared to stand up for my faith and say no because it wasn't the cool thing to do. I feared people's mean comments and gossip about me behind my back. Oh, how I wish I would have had more strength. I wish I would have sought out like-minded girls during my freshman and sophomore years and stopped being so concerned with what others would think. Why would we do things we are not okay with because of what someone else says? Who gives them the right to make decisions that could affect our life and future?

It takes time to become strong. It's one decision after another, each of them building a muscle in your heart and mind. Don't think that you are doing something wrong by refusing. That you are lame. Not cool. Not fun. You are showing such strength and courage every time you say no. You are proclaiming that you are different because you don't answer to what the world says you should do, or be like. Just like my friend said, she wanted her life to be a reflection of her heart, which is on fire for Jesus.

I know it takes a great deal of strength to say no, especially at the moment. People will laugh at you, tease you, put even more pressure on you. Staying strong is tough, but in the end, make the decision you will be proud of when you wake up the next morning. God fills us with good things, not empty calories.

I want you to, like my friend, think about the reason why you are going to parties all the time. Evaluate your heart. Are you trying to fill a void with alcohol? Does blacking out make you forget something? Are you too concerned with impressing others and fitting in? The answers to these questions are between you and God. But, if you need help or really struggle with this, please reach out to a trusted friend who does not partake in the party scene.

I know that you may grow weary of saying no and frankly it led me to many weekend nights on my own. But I kept reaching out until I found friends who had the same values as me, and slowly, that community built around me. We became each other's source of strength over those four years and spent our "party" nights going to movies, cooking desserts, crafting, and building upon our friendship. I felt like myself again, and it was wonderful.

Life Application

Verses for when you need to find Strength:

- *"For I can do everything through Christ, who gives me strength."* ~ Philippians 4:13
- *"He gives power to the weak and strength to the powerless."* ~ Isaiah 40:29
- *"That's why I take pleasure in my weaknesses, and in the insults, hardships, persecutions, and troubles that I suffer for Christ. For when I am weak, then I am strong."* ~ 2 Corinthians 12:10
- *"But those who trust in the Lord will find new strength. They will soar high on wings like eagles. They will run and not grow weary. They will walk and not faint."* ~ Isaiah 40:31

Questions to journal about:

- How do you let peer pressure influence your decisions?
- Do you look to God for your strength?
- Do you have friends who are like-minded? Why or why not?

Questions to discuss with a friend:

- Do you struggle with the party scene? If so, why?
- Do you try to fit in and do what is "cool"? Why?

- How do you feel about strength? Do you need more of it? In what specific area?

Fun tip for the week

I encourage you to make one change this week. Is there something you need to remove yourself from or stop doing? Do you want to start that blog you said you would? Start exercising more? Step out and do something brave, even if it's just speaking up more in class. Finding strength in one area will lead to strength in other areas. So make a change!

Lord, I know You can supply me with mighty strength. Thank you for being in control of my life. For never leaving me. I pray that You will speak to me as I spend time reading Your Word. Show me the areas of my life that I need to give over to You. Fill me with Your Holy Spirit, and with peace and joy. I come before You now and ask for forgiveness for the sins I have committed, for my moments of weakness. You have called me to this college for a reason. I pray that You will lead me to a Christian community. People I can do life with who love you, Jesus. I pray for strength to make the right decisions and to always choose ways to glorify You, Lord.

Amen

Chapter Eight
Patience

"But the Holy Spirit produces this kind of fruit in our lives: love, joy, peace, patience, kindness, goodness, faithfulness, gentleness, and self-control."
~ Galatians 5:22

I stared at my phone screen, waiting for those telltale three bubbles that meant a message was on its way. My roommate and I were watching *Law and Order: SVU* downstairs in our living room. But, she had her boyfriend sitting next to her, and I didn't. I looked back down at my phone and nothing. The guy I had a crush on was sporadic at best on replying to texts. He'd be silent for hours, and then my patience would reach its limit, and I would cave and text him again. I felt envy. Loneliness. Why does my roommate always have a guy to talk to, but I don't?

I went up to my room and went to bed early. My cat, Bella, was laying on my bed, curled up into a ball. I slid next to her on the bed. At that moment, with her soft purrs in my ear, I was perfectly content. I forgot about the lack of activity on my phone and felt at peace. I realized I didn't need a guy to fill this void of loneliness in my heart. I had my God, my Bella, and my dreams. Sometimes, it was nice to have a night to myself. I didn't have to impress a guy or watch a football game with him; I could do anything I wanted to do. Like watch my dramatic Netflix shows, read, write, and cuddle with my cat.

I started to dream about the kind of life I wanted, in this period while I was single. I wanted to start those ballet classes that I said I would. I wanted to focus more on doing well in school. I wanted to build my friendships more. I wanted to get more involved in my church. I was able to sleep with a peace of mind that night because I realized I already had all the freedom I needed to do the things that were important to me. **Learning how to wait patiently in my singleness was the key to enjoying the other waiting periods that came my way during college.**

Being Single

It was really hard to be single during college while my roommate and a couple of my friends had boyfriends. I craved that companionship. To have someone to talk to all the time and go on fun dates with. I wanted to fill this loneliness that I often felt while being alone. I wanted someone to hold my hand when I was sad, and celebrate with me when something exciting happened. Being single can be tough because you always want what you don't have. Never finding contentment at where you are in life. Waiting to get out of this period can seem like watching paint dry.

I found that being single can be so empowering. Yeah, girl, you have such strength and boldness inside of you! Don't let it fade just because you don't have a man in your life. This period of life is not a time to view yourself as weak, alone, or not good enough. It should be the total opposite!

Whenever a friend comes to me struggling with being single, this is what I share with them. For me, I was single all of my freshman, sophomore, and some of my junior year of college. I chased after guys, always thinking that it would turn into a relationship. After one bad breakup, I realized that I was putting too much of my worth and happiness in a guy's hands. Most college guys do not want anything serious and don't want to "settle down" during their first years of college. I wish I understood this better because it could have saved me from a lot of hurt.

They also interpret things differently from women. I remember talking to this fraternity boy I really liked. We'd text and hang out occasionally. We'd been doing this for about a month. Usually, when I hit that mark, I would become impatient wondering if the guy was ever going to turn this into a real relationship. On one particular Monday, I had stopped at Brooklyn Water Bagel to get breakfast before my class.

"What are you doing?" the frat boy asked in a text.

"I just got a Brooklyn Water Bagel! Have you ever tried it?"

"No I haven't, but it sounds really good."

"I usually go Mondays and Wednesdays before my class. Wanna go with me on Wednesday morning?"

Nothing but silence for twenty minutes. Then, he texted: "I think we're moving too fast, Jess. I don't want anything serious."

What I saw as a harmless bagel outing, he saw as commitment, responsibility, and he wanted nothing to do with it. As most women do, I took it personally. I thought he hated my personality; I wasn't pretty enough, or fun enough. It made me reevaluate who I was and why I wasn't somebody that he wanted to date.

But, how sad is that? I honestly thought that way after a guy stopped talking to me. It was like they were each taking pieces of me. My self-esteem. Confidence. Worth. Beauty. **All of these insecurities I had was like my own "service-check" light that comes on in your car, telling me that I had a lot to work on** so that I didn't let guys do this to me.

I want you to hear that it is okay to be single! Please realize that it's not about you. Do not take it so personally and start tearing down the things that make you who you are. Do not let a guy's opinion do that. College boys can be selfish, just like any of us, because we are human.

Proverbs 4:23 says to guard your heart because everything you do flows from it. Be careful with your heart, do not give it to just anyone. It is important first to give your heart to Jesus and have Him hold it in His hands. Let Jesus protect you from heartbreak and mean boys. Allow Jesus to give you your worth and beauty.

After a couple more breakups, I was so tired of the dating realm. I desperately wanted to be content in my own skin, meaning I needed to learn to love my personality, love my flaws, and most importantly, love Jesus more. So I set out to do that, and in the end, I found peace and happiness and a surety that I needed to be strong in any relationship.

What do you need to work on? Ask God to reveal it to you if you are not sure.

I learned to wait patiently during my single period by focusing my attention and energy on God and bettering myself. I knew this was a time I could never get back. A time of freedom from a relationship. I wanted to discover who I was first, so that one day when I did date a man, I could stay true to my values and beliefs, I would be able to stand on my own two feet, and I would put my joy in the Lord instead of fully on a man.

When feelings and emotions get involved, we are easily swayed to give in to temptation. That is why if you are a Christian, it is so important to seek out another Christian man to date. You will get pressured by guys to do things you vowed you never would. I don't want you to put yourself in a position where you think the only way he will love you or stay with you is to sleep with him. Because if that is the case, I am telling you to walk away, sister. His heart is not right, and he does not value your principles.

From personal experience, I would not advise using this time to talk to as many guys as you can. Be patient and wait for the right guy to come along. I encourage you to make a list. I love writing things down, especially when they are from my heart. So, make a list of the qualities you want in a future husband someday.

I encourage you to use this time to focus on your dreams, goals, career, hobbies, and friendships. What is something you have always wanted to do? Now is the time! It will make waiting so much easier when you fill your time with things you truly enjoy doing. Build up some friendships with Christian women who can help you during this time. I found that doing these things made my single period a time that was filled with joy and adventures! I want that for you too.

I encourage you to change your mindset today to being hopeful and excited for who God has planned for you to meet. **Be patient during this time, using it to grow closer to God, and become the best version of yourself.**

God's Timing

In Ecclesiastes 3, Solomon talks about how there is a time for everything. A time to plant/ harvest. Cry/ laugh. Mourn/ dance. Embrace/ turn away. Be quiet/ speak. It would not be healthy for us to only stay in a mourning state, and never get the joy to dance again. There is a season for both of these things. It is important to learn to embrace and experience the season that you are in.

"Yet God has made everything beautiful in its own time…" (Ecclesiastes 3:11a)

We experience waiting periods at different times in life, but we must remember that God orchestrates all of that. He knows the exact moment that we need things. **That is why you will never stay in one season forever—God will always bring you to the other side of it.** In His timing, which I know can be hard to wait for.

I recently heard the term "microwave generation." Our society has become so impatient that we stand and stare at the microwave, counting down the seconds. Fast food still isn't convenient enough for us because of the long lines. We expect everything to happen right when we want it to. We don't want to wait. Can you relate?

"Microwave Christians" get frustrated with God when He doesn't answer their prayers right away. They want their problems to disappear fast.

Being content with where you are in life, right this moment, will help you become a more patient person. I know this can be hard when the future can seem so exciting. You may think that once you do ___ your life can finally begin.

Being content means to be grateful for what you do have, and not always desiring more.

Whatever waiting period you find yourself in right now, it is important to find contentment during that. I want you to understand that God is with you. He knows what He is doing. If it feels like you have been waiting for years, and maybe you actually have, hold on to your hope and trust that God will see you through it. He promises us that.

Not all waiting periods should be viewed as bad. That is the problem we humans have with patience. We don't like it. My single period was a blessing of time. The thing is, you won't be stuck there forever, so do not let that time be wasted. Life still goes on, so we must keep living and focus our mind more on God than on the waiting.

If you find yourself in this place, remember that God is not bound by the same time that we are. We only see a glimmer of reality, while God sees our past, present, and future all intertwined in a perfect design. While we pray now for something in the future, our mighty God is already there. God's timing is always perfect.

We must be careful here because we could miss the blessing God intends for us by taking matters into our own hands. God has a Plan A for our lives, but sometimes we end up with Plan B because of our own impatient nature. We try to make things happen by ourselves without consulting God on the matter.

I have done this with my major a couple of times during college. Maybe that's why I changed it so much. I almost missed out on God's Plan A for my life, by going to nursing school. I was about to resist all the red flags God showed me. I had this idea cemented in my mind that I wanted to make happen because society told me I needed a stable job.

Patience means giving up the control on our plans, lists, and ideas over to God. It is so hard to do this because we're used to being in control. Day-to-day decisions we have control over, so why not our future milestones? That is because God has not made us all-knowing, and He has done this for our own good. We do not know what is best for us—only God does. We often let emotions or opinions sway our judgment when it comes to big choices. Remember that God is in control, plain and simple.

If you really struggle with control, as I have, pray to God and be honest with Him. Open up your hands, releasing and surrendering control over to God. To be patient is to hand God the steering wheel. Let Him have your worries over what to do next. I know you may ask yourself, how can I mark up my calendar if I don't know what will happen tomorrow? Well, that is where trust comes in. We must surrender control and then trust in God. Patience comes from trusting in God's plan for your life.

Look back over times where God did steer you in the right direction, even when you thought otherwise. That creates trust in your heart, which multiplies your faith. You can feel at peace knowing that God is in control of the answers, not you. I'll let you in on a secret: His answer is always correct.

When your patience is being tested, remember to trust in the promises that the Lord gives us in His Word and surrender your control. Allow God to use the waiting periods in your life to fulfill the plan that He has for you. God is always at work to bring you through one season to the next. Believe that, and be patient!

Life Application

Verses to help you with Patience:

- *"Yet God has made everything beautiful in its own time. He has planted eternity in the human heart, but even so, people cannot see the whole scope of God's work from beginning to end. So I concluded there is nothing better than to be happy and enjoy ourselves as long as we can."* - Ecclesiastes 3:11-12
- *"We also pray that you will be strengthened with all His glorious power, so you will have all the endurance and patience you need. May you be filled with joy, always thanking the Father. He has enabled you to share in the inheritance that belongs to His people, who live in the light."* - Colossians 1:11-12
- *"Such things were written in the Scriptures long ago to teach us. And the Scripture gives us hope and encouragement as we wait patiently for God's promises to be fulfilled."* - Romans 15:4

Questions to journal about:

- Do you consider yourself a patient person? What things in your life are you most impatient about?
- Which of these verses resonates with you?
- What are you holding onto to, that you can't let go of control? Is there some fear at the root of that?

Questions to discuss with a friend:

- How do you feel about waiting periods? Are you in one now? Does it make you scared?
- What is one area in your life where you are consistently impatient?
- Are you a control freak? Why or why not? How does that make things better or worse for you?

Fun tip for the week:

This week I want you to journal about a waiting period or trying time in your life. List all the ways that God sent you signs that it was all going to be okay, that He was working on it. Look back at that with perspective, then apply it to your current situations.

I pray for patience this week. Forgive me for not trusting in Your plans for my life. Please give me that restful spirit that I find when I truly trust You. I do not want to be overwhelmed by worry any longer. I release all my stress over school, perfectionism, friendships, and purpose over to You, Lord. Fill me with Your strength and endurance to be patient in hard times. Help me to be grateful in the space between and to see the signs You are sending to me. I know Your timing is perfect, and I will rest on that today. Your will be done, Lord, on earth as it is in Heaven.

Amen

Chapter Nine
Truths

"So faith comes from hearing, that is, hearing the Good News about Christ." ~ Romans 10:17

In the last semester of my senior year as a college student, I joined a women's Bible study through Action Church. The first night, the Bible study leader talked about how the power of the Word of God would change our lives this semester. I didn't quite know what she meant by this, but that radical change that she spoke about sounded enticing. Tears were shed on that first night as girl after girl started to open up. Every single Monday night that we met, without a doubt, one story that a girl shared I had either been there or was going through it, too. We all got to experience God working in our lives.

My whole mindset on what the Bible represented changed during that semester. What once was just a book that I frequently read to feel better, turned into a powerful tool, weapon, and a priority to me. It formed the basis of the truths in my life. Let me share with you how, so that you may look at the Bible like you have never done before!

In the Beginning

"In the beginning the Word already existed. The Word was with God, and the Word was God." (John 1:5) Jesus and the Word of God are one in the same! How cool is that? The words that we read in the Bible manifested into Jesus when He took on flesh. We all have the power of Jesus in our hands.

As Christians, we have been told to read our Bibles every day. Too often we start to turn this into a chore instead of a resource. Maybe you are just going through the motions as you read that one chapter every day, which you think will fill you up with all you need to have a good day. If this is you, then you are missing the big picture. The Word of God has the power to make real changes in your life. **If we read with purpose and openness, the Living Word will come alive and bring you answers, hope, and fulfillment.**

You know those hefty textbooks that you are required to buy for your classes? Yeah, the ones that are "required" but you never crack open the whole semester? Or if you're an English major like me, you are forced to read lengthy literature stories in these thick books that weigh more than a small child. You fall asleep while reading, wishing you were doing anything else. Your mind kind of shuts off and if I asked you what you just read, you probably wouldn't be able to tell me.

The Bible can become like a textbook to us. If we are reading it with our mind shut off, just going through the motions to "get it done," then we are not allowing the Bible to work in our lives fully. We are not opening the door to our hearts to hear the Spirit of God speak.

Do you need to change your attitude towards the Bible?

Why is it that we can quote song lyrics and lines from a movie so easily, but verses from the Bible sometimes make us draw a blank?

There are certain things the body needs to keep operating properly, like food and water. I know in college, a lot of times this food means pizza, cereal, and ramen noodles. It wasn't the healthiest diet, and when I ate like that, I didn't feel as strong or energized as when I did eat healthy. It's the same with what we put in our minds and hearts. Our spirit needs proper nourishment to work well. The Word of God can provide those nutrients that our mind and soul need. Truly having the Word of God come alive in your life, means being mindful of it and able to remember His promises. (For more information on quiet time, refer to the Additional Resources page in the back of the book.)

Being mindful means working on your relationship with God. He is available to talk with you 24/7. Get in the habit of praising Him when something good happens, and sharing with Him whatever worries may be dwelling in your mind. As I started doing that, **I saw how God could turn my day around with a simple prayer.** When I left class, overwhelmed with all the studying I had left to do that day, I would talk to God about it. The work didn't necessarily get easier, but my mind was more peaceful and ready to focus.

When the words in a sermon speak to you, or you hear a Bible verse at exactly the right time, that is called the Living Word of God coming alive. I now use the Bible as my tool, when I need to seek after God's truths. Whatever trial I am going through, whatever lie I start to believe, I look to the Bible to tell me the truth. I have learned not to trust other people's opinions or even my own. God's Word is the best way for me to believe something about myself, like truth #1.

Truth #1: You are beautiful.

"I praise you because I am __________ and __________ made; your works are __________, I know that full well." ~ Psalm 139:14 NIV

My sister and brother-in-law recently opened up a donut shop, The Donut Experiment on Clearwater Beach. I've realized that just as no two donuts look exactly the same, neither do we. Donuts are unique in their own way, while still being sweet on the inside. We are not meant to look like our female peers. We are all different in shape, size, and appearance, just like donuts.

Just because you don't look like __________ (insert the girl's name who pops in your head) does not mean that you are not beautiful. You are unique and beautiful in your own way. I believe true beauty comes from within. When we have a kind, genuine heart, it radiates out of us onto others. This heart comes from having the Holy Spirit living inside of us.

Remember, we are wonderfully made in God's image. **God doesn't make mistakes, so that means He didn't make a mistake creating you, either.**

"For we are God's masterpiece. He has created us anew in Christ Jesus, so we can do the good things He planned for us long ago." (Ephesians 2:10) The word "masterpiece" is defined as an artist's best piece of work. So that means that God views every one of us as His best piece of work.

During college, your self-confidence, self-esteem, worth, and appearance will all be judged by girls, boys, social media, and by your own self. Your worth and beauty should be found in God alone, and not in the opinions of others. We seek other outlets of approval like our Instagram likes rather than turning to the truth in the Living Word. When you feel less than beautiful or unworthy, look to God to remind you how unique and wonderfully made you are. He loves you so much. You are His daughter after all, and there is so much power in that!

I love this quote that I saw scrolling through my Pinterest feed one day; "On the darkest days, when I feel inadequate, unloved, and unworthy. I remember whose daughter I am and I straighten my crown." Go back to when you were a little girl, trying on your mom's dresses and jewelry. I'm sure you looked in the mirror and said something like *I look so beautiful!* I know I did! We need to start viewing ourselves as beautiful again. Go ahead, straighten your crown. You are a princess!

Truth #2: Intentionality through kindness.

> "For whatever is in your _____ determines what you say. A good person produces ____ things from the treasury of a _____ heart, and an evil person produces ____ things from the treasury of an _____ heart." ~ Matthew 12:34b-35

There is power in words. As a writer, I firmly believe that words can change people's mood, circumstances, and lives. We must speak kind words of encouragement toward others. Our day-to-day speech is like a looking glass into our hearts. What does your daily speech say about you?

The more of Jesus we have in our hearts, the more love we will show others. Our speech will be filled with grace, encouragement, love, and power. The other thing about words is that they can stay with us for a long time. You may be thinking of a situation where really hurtful words were spoken to you, or maybe you remember the first time you heard "I love you." Our speech can tear others down or build them up with encouragement.

As you go through college, you will treasure those words of encouragement when you needed them the most. My parents and friends often tried to fill me up with encouragement before I took a big test or before one of my volleyball games. Their words, coupled with the knowledge that God is with me, initiated a spark inside my soul.

You can be this source of encouragement to others with kind words. I labeled this section "Intentionality through kindness," because I believe living an intentional life will bring you so much more joy than living a life to please others.

Living an intentional life simply means to think about others before yourself, and to then be kind with your words and actions. Acts of kindness go such a long way in brightening someone's day. You know how it feels to be on the receiving end of these, so I encourage you to be intentional and do the same. You never know the impact you can make on someone's life until you let God take you there.

Personally, I seek friendships where we are both intentional in each other's lives. Ephesians 4:32 says, "Instead, be kind to each other, tenderhearted, forgiving one another just as God through Christ has forgiven you." I love the word tenderhearted—it means to have a kind, gentle, and sentimental nature about you. That is how I want to be described. I want to leave a handprint on someone's life. Knowing that I helped at least one person get through something tough or even helped them celebrate a triumph is so rewarding. Others will notice this difference in you. Kindness is infectious! It draws people to you because you make others feel good.

So be kind to each other. We all need to be shown love and encouragement through the ups and downs of life!

Truth #3: You can overcome the enemy.

> "That at the name of _____ every knee should bow, in heaven and on earth and under the earth."
> ~ Philippians 2:10

It is written in the Bible that we have authority over the devil. Drop the microphone…is this true?

This realization changed how I went about the disappointments and trials of my days! I knew that I didn't have to entertain and give in to the devil's attacks. I could rise above them. Luke 10:18-19 says, "'Yes', He told them, 'I saw Satan fall from heaven like lightning! Look, I have given you authority over all the power of the enemy, and you can walk among snakes and scorpions and crush them. Nothing will injure you.'" Jesus dying for our sins on the cross was the ultimate defeat over the devil. As Christians, we can now overcome the lies that the devil tries to derail us with.

Whenever something big was coming up, like a date, a volleyball tournament, or a final, the devil would hit me hard with his arrows. I had to fervently pray against the negative and doubtful thoughts that would try to flood my mind. When we experience a lot of stress and pressures, and those negative thoughts try to take root, we need to be aware which messages are from the enemy and fight back.

He can be really subtle and whisper a thousand excuses for your thoughts—you got cut off in traffic, your friend was mean, you're feeling hormonal. We must recognize what the devil is trying to do before he gains the power over us. As Christians, we are engaged in a spiritual battle, and the weapons we use to fight back are not from this world, but from God. If you have never read about God's armor that He gives us, take a look at Ephesians 6:10-18.

Hear this: you can overcome trials, setbacks, and negative thoughts by releasing them into the Lord's hands. I want you to declare out loud that the devil has no place in your mind or your heart. You have not laid out the welcome mat for him. You have not invited him in, push him out. I want you to say "In Jesus' name, you have no power over my dreams, my family, my heart, so get out, devil. Nice try, but you are not winning today. I have the power over you! So get out!" Yell it, scream it if you want (maybe when you aren't in class or the supermarket) but always stand tall, pray and banish whatever lie is in your head.

I like to find a specific verse for whatever I am really struggling with. When I was in my last semester, I really struggled with my future career. I didn't know what I would be doing after graduation. I had expectant hope most days, but oh, how the devil tried to break me down. During my morning devotions one day, I read Proverbs 3:5-6. That passage says to trust in the Lord and not my own understanding. I drew from that verse in those moments when I doubted my future. I would repeat the verse again and again, until I actually believed it.

That is the power of God's Word! Allow it to work in your life today. Meditate and study God's promises, so you don't have to fall victim to the enemy and the trials of this world.

Life Application

Below is the Armor of God from Ephesians 6:14-17. Use these as an outline for prayer, to start each day in preparation to fight against the enemy.

- Belt of Truth. *Defeats the devil's lies with God's truth.*
- Breastplate of Righteousness. *Protects our heart and reminds us that our approval comes from the Lord.*
- Shoes of Peace. *Motivates us to continue to proclaim the Good News and true peace that comes from God.*
- Shield of Faith. *Protects us from the devil's arrows and helps us see that ultimate victory can be ours.*
- Helmet of Salvation. *Protects our mind from doubting God and His promises.*
- Sword of the Spirit. *Helps us actively trust in the truth of God's Word.*

Questions to journal about:

- How do you view yourself in the mirror? Do you have a negative or positive self-image?
- Does your daily speech reflect that God lives inside of you?
- Are you intentional in your words and actions?
- Are you reading the Bible as a chore or out of a desire to grow closer to God?

Questions to discuss with a friend:

- ❀ Do you say things that you quickly regret afterwards? How do you try to stop doing that?
- ❀ Do you want a friend who is intentional in your life? How would you want them to be intentional?
- ❀ What does the Bible mean to you?
- ❀ What is one truth that you need to search for in God's Word today?

Fun tip for the week:

I want you to write out a Declaration of Blessing this week. Write down all the ways that you are blessed. (I'll give you an example of some in the prayer below) Hang it on your mirror. Put it somewhere that you will read it every day. And then believe what it says!

Thank you for blessing me with the ability to touch other people with my words. Thank you for blessing me with the means to go to college and get an education. I am so happy that I can have victory over the devil because sometimes his attacks really bring me down. But I am ready to fight back with Your Word and help. I am so blessed to be one of Your daughters. I pray that I will view myself like You do, Lord. I know I am beautifully and wonderfully made in Your eyes. I pray for strength and perseverance today as I overcome my daily struggles. I will trust in Your name, Jesus, and proclaim victory today.

Amen

Chapter Ten
Peace

"I am leaving you with a gift - peace of mind and heart. And the peace I give is a gift the world cannot give. So don't be troubled or afraid."
~ John 14:27

I sat on my big beach towel alone, watching as the sun rose from the horizon. I had my Bible, journal, and my coffee cup beside me. The sound of the waves continually crashing, relaxed my whole body and mind. There was only one older couple next to me fishing; otherwise, it felt like I had the whole beach to myself. I was in my senior year of college and found myself in desperate need of answers from God.

I needed direction in the right career I should pursue, in the timing of how different things were going to play out. I hit a point where I didn't know what to do, so I turned to the One who could give me that peace that I longed for. The best way I was able to hear God speaking to me was when I was alone and often, in nature. I felt God's presence with each wave that broke, and in how the sun rose every morning creating a scene that looked like it was hand painted.

What does this quiet spot look like for you?

My favorite way to share the worries on my heart with God is to write them down in my journal. I feel like I am physically handing it over to God. I can meditate on everything I write down, focus my attention on it, and allow God to fill me with peace. That feeling that everything is going to be okay and going to work out. I am at peace knowing that I am actively searching and listening to God's will.

Outer Peace

You want to feel that outer peace in your life. To be happy with where you are in life and know you are on the right path. Sometimes, this can be hard when you never think you are content with your current season. Could it be that you are looking in the wrong places?

In TV shows and movies, they make all kinds of jobs look so glamorous and fun. Shows like *Grey's Anatomy, Law and Order,* or *Suits* make being a doctor or lawyer seem empowering and fun. I remember watching those shows, and something inside of me said *well, maybe I should pursue that. Or that. Or maybe that.* Media, other people, and things we read can have a significant impact on our thoughts, and sway us in different directions.

I had my head up in the clouds for most of college. Jumping from one idea to the next. And then one Sunday morning at church, the sermon was on dreams. I sat up straighter, got my notebook and pen out, and zoned in on every word. I remember thinking this is the day I learn what I'm supposed to do.

That sermon opened my eyes to a new way to view dreams. The pastor wanted us to think about our passions.

What set our heart on fire? What did we do on a regular basis that we truly enjoyed? What were our talents and gifts? He wanted us to dig deeper into what we cared about and what made us happy.

I made a list, titled, "What am I passionate about?" Then I started listing things I loved to do. Think about your hobbies, what you could do every day that you never seem to get tired of. Do you like animals, helping others, or dancing? Write down everything that comes to mind.

The second list was, "What are my strengths?" This means what your gifts and talents are. What do you excel at? We all have different strengths, and it is important to narrow in on your own.

The third list was "What are my dreams?" Write down every dream big and small. It can be like your bucket list. One of mine is to be on the show *So You Think You Can Dance*. What are yours? Have fun with it!

When you think about what your future career will be someday, it might be something that you are already doing. For me, I have been reading and writing ever since middle school. For my sister, we would always play classroom growing up and then she became a teacher.

My sister explained to me how she was nervous about starting her teaching internships in her senior year of college. Some of the thoughts running through her head were: *Will I have a ride to get there because I don't have a car? What school will I be placed at? Will the internship teacher be nice and helpful in my teaching journey? Will I still love teaching after interning in real-life classrooms?*

She said, "I reached a point where I was overwhelmed and anxious. I decided to surrender these worries and fears to God. After I prayed that, I truly felt the peace of God. I knew He would take care of me and that He had a plan." Those internships showed my sister that her heart was in teaching because she loved every minute of being around the children and watching them grow.

She said, "**You'll know when the peace is from God because the worries and doubts disappear and don't seem important anymore.**"

I love that statement! When you feel peace from God about a big decision, all those doubts that you had worried about will disappear out of your mind. I had a similar situation happen to me in my senior year.

I once again had to tell my parents I was changing my major. This time it was back to what I began college with, English. My CNA (Certified Nursing Assistant) job opened my eyes to the reality of being a nurse. My "dream" job quickly turned into an awful time filled with anxiety and tears. It was clear as day to me through that job that nursing was not the right career for me. Nursing was "my" dream, not God's. I honestly knew this in my heart, but of course variables still led me to chase after it. Job security. Good pay. God gives us free will here on earth, and He will do the same with you on your journey. If you want to be a painter on Tuesday and then Friday you decide to switch to becoming a professional ballerina, God will let you. But He will always bring you to where you are supposed to be if you go off course, just like me.

God gave me peace in the midst of my uncertainty that I was making the right decision in putting this nursing dream to rest. I no longer had to be somebody that I wasn't. I chose nursing out of fear of failing in my career. I thought that this was the only job for me to make money.

It wasn't until I put down my own understanding, and listened to the signs that God gave me that I found that outer peace in my life. I found so much joy and happiness being back in English. My dad always says, "If you love what you do, you won't work a day in your life."

I fell back in love with writing during my last semester of college; once I followed God's dream for my life. I started a blog the day I took my last final. Then shortly after that, I wrote this book that is in your hands right now. Since I was a little girl in middle school, with my nose always in books, I knew I wanted to write a book of my very own. That was over eleven years ago. Was pursuing a writing career risky? Yes. Would this journey be hard? Yes. Is it worth it? Absolutely yes.

I encourage you to find that outer peace in your life by following what makes your heart happy and where God is leading you. **Remember to find this we must still ourselves before the Lord and actively listen and seek after His Will.** He will reveal it to you by giving you that inner peace.

Inner Peace

You know when you think about an upcoming test, date, or even surgery and all the worry and anxiety that you should be feeling is absent? Instead, you feel at ease about it; no anxiety is making your body warm and tingling. That is inner peace that you feel.

Psalm 32:8 says, "I will guide you along the best pathway for your life. I will advise you and watch over you." This is God speaking to us in this verse. When doubts and worries come, and you don't know which decision to make, be in constant prayer, asking God to reveal to you which path to take. Whenever I am praying about a big decision, I feel an overwhelming peace when I know I should say yes or no. I would suggest going somewhere quiet. I love being in nature to talk with God! When I was in college, it was hard sometimes to find that stillness. I really had to make the time and get away from my townhouse. I would go to a local park, or

I would watch the sunrise, like my story at the beginning of the chapter.

I was at the beach watching the sunrise when I made my three soul-searching lists. That time spent in the quiet, pouring out to God my hopes and dreams, I truly felt peace within me in the direction I should take.

This peace that I so strongly feel comes from one place. Jesus. Once I accepted Jesus Christ as my Savior, I could feel the Holy Spirit living inside of me.

God sacrificed His only Son for you. For me. Wow. Close your eyes and think about that. God loves you that much!

> *"For God loved the world so much that He gave His one and only Son, so that everyone who believes in Him will not perish but have eternal life. God sent His Son into the world not to judge the world, but to save the world through Him."* - John 3:16-17

If you are not a Christian, to believe means to put your trust and confidence in Jesus for He alone can save you. Save you from your fears. From your worries. He did not come to judge you and what you have done, but to offer you everlasting life. To allow you first to forgive yourself, so then you can receive God's forgiveness. All we have to do is believe and ask Jesus into our lives. To put down our old selves, repent of the sins we have made, and accept the forgiveness that God offers us.

No good deeds or being a good person will get you into heaven. Jesus just wants your heart. I will personally share with you, that when you do this, I pray it will be the same for you as for me—you will feel like a new person, like air has finally been returned to your lungs, peace overwhelms your whole being, and you have no reason to fear the things of this world, because Jesus has overcome them. We just need to trust in Him. (For more information on how to accept Jesus into your life, refer to the Additional Resources page at the end of the book.)

I never felt completely alone throughout college because I knew Jesus was always watching over me, and carrying me when I felt too weak to walk. I could defeat the lies I heard from Satan because I knew the truth that God tells us in His Word. My fears and worries disappeared as I gave them over to God. I found the courage to take opportunities that came my way during college by asking and trusting in God. He supplied me with the strength to stand firm in my values and make good decisions. I was able to be a more patient person as I waited on God because I knew He had a plan for my life as He promises in Jeremiah 29:11. Lastly, peace. That was one of the best gifts God gave me while I experienced many trials and big decisions. I focused my attention and heart on Jesus, and I saw Him work in miraculous ways. I would sit back with a sigh of relief, thanking God again and again for how He brought people into my life, gave me life-changing opportunities, and helped me overcome my weaknesses.

I am such a different woman than I was when I started college. God truly blossomed me into the woman I am right now. I'll let you in on a secret—it is because I let Him. I allowed Him to work in my life because I wanted to be the best version of myself. Of course, I am still learning and growing every single day as I face new seasons and journeys. But, that foundation is there. Jesus is my foundation.

College showed me who I was through so many different situations. I saw things I did not like, and a lot that I did like. Ultimately, I was able to grow from all of it. Those experiences taught me to be strong, fearless, and to always stay true to myself.

I hope by reading this book, you can see that through anything you experience in life, God is always with you. He wants you to embrace everything that college has to offer. I want you to realize this power and strength inside of you. You can do great things! **You are beautiful, strong, able, and worth it.** Don't let the hard trials of this world weigh you down, find renewed hope and joy in the goodness of God!

And finally, blossom from one journey to the next. I know you can.

Life Application

My four favorite verses that were my rock throughout college:

- Jeremiah 29:11. *For I know the plans I have for you, says the Lord. They are plans for good and not for disaster, to give you a future and a hope.*
- Philippians 4:6-7. *Don't worry about anything; instead, pray about everything. Tell God what you need, and thank Him for all He has done. Then you will experience God's peace, which exceeds anything we can understand. His peace will guard your hearts and minds as you live in Christ Jesus.*
- Ephesians 2:8. *God saved you by His grace when you believed. And you can't take credit for this; it is a gift from God.*
- Proverbs 3:5-6. *Trust in the Lord with all your heart; do not depend on your own understanding. Seek His Will in all you do, and He will show you which path to take.*

Questions to journal about:

- Do you experience peace in your life?
- What has God opened your eyes to through this book?
- What pulled at your heart the most?

Questions to discuss with a friend:

- What chapter spoke to you the most?
- What story in this book resonated with you?
- Do you feel God blossoming you into your true self?

Fun tip for the week:

This week I want you to create that quiet space. Go to a park, the beach, or even a chair in your backyard. Read your Bible, journal, or simply be still. Spend time with God and allow Him to give you clarity and inner peace!

Thank you for allowing me to pursue my dreams here on this earth. Thank you for gently leading me in the right direction. I pray for continued strength and courage through my many journeys of life. I know You will go with me Lord, as I discover who I am and what I am meant to do. Thank you for all You have done and will do for me, Lord.

Amen

Additional Resources

How to accept Jesus into your life:

Do you believe that Jesus is the Christ, the Son of the living God?

Do you believe that Jesus died, was buried, and rose again on the third day?

Do you believe that by Jesus dying on the cross, He paid the penalty for your sin?

Do you believe it is by faith that we are saved and not by our good deeds?

Are you willing to allow Jesus Christ to be Lord (leader) of your life?

You can do this right now by saying this prayer below.

Salvation Prayer:

O God, I am a sinner. I confess that I have sinned against You in words, thought, and deed. I want to turn away from it now. Please forgive me of all my wrongdoings and let me live in relationship with You. I believe Jesus Christ is Your Son; I believe He died on the cross for my sins and You raised Him to life. I want to trust Jesus as my Savior and follow Him as my Lord from this day forward. Lord, I put my trust in You and surrender my life to You. Please come into my life and fill me with Your Holy Spirit.

Amen.

As a child of God:

1. All of your sins are forgiven ~ past, present, & future.
2. You have become a new creation and have begun a new life in Christ.
3. Heaven has become your eternal home.
4. You are now empowered by the Holy Spirit.
5. You can experience peace that transcends all understanding.

Next Steps:

1. Christian baptism ~ an outward expression of your inward decision.
2. Join a local church that gets its authority from the Bible.
3. Pray daily.
4. Read your Bible and devotions daily.
5. Find a Christian woman to be your mentor.

How to have quiet time:

Spending time with God causes the pressures of life to dissipate. It will help you develop a personal closeness with God.

There are four main parts to your quiet time:

Devotions:

- Here are some that I have used:
  - *Jesus Calling* by Sarah Young
  - *Starting Your Day Right* by Joyce Meyers
  - *Beautiful Now* by Stasi Eldredge
- When you read a devotional, it is important to look up the Bible verses they may give.

Bible:

- I recommend the *Life Application Bible NLT*.
  - This study Bible explains each verse to you in the footnotes, so that it is easy to understand. I love that part!
- "Study this Book of Instruction continually. Meditate on it day and night, so you will be sure to obey everything written in it. Only then will you prosper and succeed in all you do." (Joshua 1:8)

Prayer:

- Prayer is a conversation with God.
  - You can carry on continuous, open-ended conversations with God throughout your day. You can talk to Him about whatever you are feeling or thinking at that moment.

- We can boldly approach God's throne.
    - "So let us come boldly to the throne of our gracious God. There we will receive His mercy, and we will find grace to help us when we need it most." (Hebrews 4:16)
- At the end of your quiet time, talk to God about your day. About the concerns on your heart. He is always there to listen!

Meditate:

- The Bible repeatedly urges us to meditate on who God is, what He has done, and what He has said.
- Meditation is simply focused thinking. When you think about God's Word over and over in your mind, that's meditation. We must be still so that we can hear from God.
- Prayer lets you speak to God; meditation lets God speak to you.